MY SON'S STORY

A CRITICAL STUDY

Nadine Gordimer's

MY SON'S STORY

A CRITICAL STUDY

Nandita Sinha

abc
asia book club
an international publishing house

Published by
Asia Book Club
New Delhi 110 058
Ph. 9818755529

ISBN: 81-7851-018-9

Printed at Chaman Offset Press, New Delhi 110 002

Contents

Nadine Gordimer: Biography

Nadine Gordimer was born on November 20, 1923, into a well-off family in Springs, Transvaal, an East Rand gold mining town outside Johannesburg.[1] Her father, Isidore Gordimer, was a Jewish jeweller originally from Lithunia. Her mother, Nan Myers Gordimer, was of British descent. She attended convent school for a while, but what distinguished Nadine Gordimer's youth from that of similar white children in comparable small mining towns was not the ethos of her family, but the fact that her mother took her out of school at the age of eleven on the pretext of a heart ailment and kept her at home until she was sixteen. Hence she had little formal schooling, and lived entirely within the social orbit of her parents, particularly her mother. Trailing her mother to afternoon teas, she spent her time observing and mimicking the people she would later portray so astutely—the "well-meaning," members of white South African society. In her isolation and loneliness, she retreated into herself, reading voraciously and thereby discovered a world more to her liking—the world of ideas. She said that "it was learning to write that sent [her] falling, falling through the surface of 'the South African way of life' . . . and the shameful enormity of the colour bar."[2] But it was not until she began reading Katherine Mansfield, a New Zealander, that she could identify a colonial voice in literature and understood that "it was possible to be a writer even if you didn't live in

England." Nadine Gordimer credits books with being the developing force in her life, for they provided a view of the world her personal life did not reveal. She writes:

> I was born in a small town on a high plateau in Africa. It was one of the towns that had grown up along the fold reef that has made South Africa the richest country on the continent. Around me were streets of bungalow houses, my horizon was flat veldt, the natural features of my landscape were mine headgear and manmade hills of yellow sand from the mines. This was not the Africa I read about and saw pictures of in books: When I was a child it seemed to me that I lived in the most ignored and therefore what must be the most uninteresting part of the whole world. I wrote from the age of nine or ten but it was only when I was about twenty that I realized that what I was writing about was exotic—the life of the mining towns scratching the marks of a thin European civilisation whose shabbier conventions we were taught to reproduce, and the black men from the mines, familiarly seen walking from their clay-dressed hair, their anklets and blankets, were to us no more than the Sakabula birds with their long tails whose calls, like the speech of the men, we didn't expect to understand. We had black nannies and servants at home, of course, of the tame canary breed, but they—in our presence anyway—gave back a third-hand reflection of the genteel 'European' ways we ourselves had second-hand.
>
> I am the daughter of a Jewish watch-maker who emigrated to Africa from a Baltic town when he was thirteen, and my mother was born in England. I had a scrappy and uninspiring minimal education and a deadly dull colonial social background, and at an early age turned to books for all that that background did not offer me. Life was prefigured in them; without knowing quite how I should bring this about, I

> felt that I should live it for myself someday. I began, quite unconsciously, through writing; passing from the passive act of reading to the creative act of writing brought me to life. Walls fell down; one of the biggest was the colour bar, I discovered that although the law of my country and the custom of the white people kept them huddled together with their skirts drawn up away from what Africa really is, I in myself was free of their prejudices and their fears. I was not merely part of a suburban white life aping Europe; I lived with and among a variety of colours and kinds of people. This discovery was a joyous personal one, not a political one, at first; but, of course, as time has gone by it has hardened into a sense of political opposition to abusive white power. The core of it remains a personal freedom, to me.
>
> I wrote stories long before I began to write novels and continue to write both. Out of the sixty or more stories I have written, there are some that satisfy me, but I have not written, yet, the novel I should like to write and perhaps may never be capable of. I am not interested in repeating, with variations, what i know I can do as a writer; with each book I want to attempt to grasp what has eluded me before. I never discuss work in progress and am inarticulate in discussion of literary theory as applied to my own writing. But I have written elsewhere and will repeat: I think that a writer's purpose is to make sense of life. Even the most esoteric of linguistic innovations, the wildest experiments with form, are an expression of this purpose. The only dictum I always remember is Andrè Gide's dictum—"Salvation, for the writer, lies in being sincere even against one's better judgement." The ideal way to write is as if oneself and one's readers were already dead.[3]

In another essay recalling her childhood, Gordimer describes the strange landscape of the East Rand, the richest mining region in the world It was a bleak and eerie scene, with its man-made mountains of waste material, cyanide sand hills and smouldering coal dust dumps. The town was equally barren, causing Gordimer to observe: "We children simply took it for granted that beauty—hills, trees, buildings of elegance—was not a thing to be expected of ordinary everyday life."

In an interview to the Boston Globe, she spoke of the conflicts that arose within her as she became aware of the injustices of the society around her.

> You were being taught as a child that it's wrong to tell lies but the whole society is a lie, the life you were living was a lie. The convent school I went to was for whites only. When I got pocket money on Saturday and went to the movies, only whites could go. Most important, the local public library—I would never have been a writer without it—was open only to white people.
>
> So wasn't this privilege a big lie? There was this enormous lie and all the little lies that justified it: "Blacks don't really need the things that we need." So the more you grew up in that society, the more you started to question, the more you fell through one layer of lies to the next. And to find the bits of truth that were there, you had to dig into yourself, pass judgement on your parents, on everything that makes your life stable, the very structure of your life.[4]

A new world opened to Gordimer in 1949 when she began taking courses in Johannesburg at the University of Witwaterstrand. There she mingled with musicians, journalists, and writers, crossing for the first time the colour line that segregated blacks from whites. Her own precocious talent laid open the larger world beyond. As she read the philosophies of Marxism, nationalism and existentialism, she began to question the social structure of apartheid. She also became involved with the political and cultural movement of the Sophiatown renaissance, which produced the literary journal *Drum.*

Her first story "Come Again Tomorrow" appeared in the Johannesburg magazine *Forum* when she was only fourteen and other stories followed. In 1951, the highly esteemed *New Yorker* published the first of many of her stories that appeared in the well-known literary magazine, as well as in *Harper*'s and other American magazines. These stories were first collected in *Face to Face* (1949) and later in *The Soft Voice of the Serpent* (1952) and quickly established her reputation as an accomplished short story writer. They were followed by 12 novels and 13 short story collections, as well as numerous essays, collected into four volumes, in which Gordimer has commented on the politics of writing and the evolution of leftist political action. She has also written on aesthetics and literary criticism and on her own travels around a rapidly changing continent. In her autobiographical essays she probes and scrutinizes the evolution of her own thinking—always with a self-critical gaze at her own position as a white woman. Her other credits include screenplays for television dramas and the script for the film 'Frontiers' and a documentary film entitled 'Hanging on a Sunrise.'

She has been awarded honorary degrees from universities all over the world and is Vice-President of International PEN as well as executive member of the Congress of South African Writers.

Her status as one of the major writers of the century has been confirmed by the many prizes and honours that have come her way—the W.H. Smith Literary Award for her short story collection *Friday's Footprint* (1960), the James Tait Black Memorial Prize in Britain and the CNA Literary Prize in South Africa for *A Guest of Honour* (1970), the Booker Prize for *The Conservationist* (1974), the CNA Prize in South Africa for *Burger's Daughter* (1979)—culminating in the award of the Nobel Prize for Literature in 1991, where the judges declared: "Through her magnificent epic writing she has—in the words of Alfred Nobel—been of very great benefit to humanity." She shared her $ 985,000 cash award with the mainly black Congress of South African Writers and the African National Congress to promote libraries and scholarships. However, in 1998, Gordimer declined to be short-listed for the Orange Award on the grounds that it was restricted to women writers.

In spite of her taking part in demonstrations, giving speeches and travelling round the world in support of good causes, Gordimer is an intensely private person. For her, the hardest part has been the political activism, she has said. But without it, "I couldn't have retained my self-respect or been at peace with myself in South Africa." Hence she endured the black decades, refusing to move abroad as others did, out of commitment to black liberation and also for the sake of her own creativity and that of black South African writers who were silenced, for whom she had to speak. "I always had the feeling that to go into exile is to lose your place in the world, your responsibility, your source. To be a good writer, you have to be a citizen."

In 1998, she was appointed Goodwill Ambassador for the United Nations Development Program's Decade for the Eradication of Poverty.

NOTES

1. See www.nobel.se/literature/articles/wastberg/indexhtml
2. In her essay "The Bolter and the Invincible Summer," 1963.
3. From John Wakeman, ed., *World Authors 1950-1970* (New York: The H.W. Wilson Company, 1975), pp. 577-78.
4. Boston Globe interview by David Mehergan http://www.boston.com/globe/search/stories/nobel/1994/1994d.html

Apartheid and South Africa

The first Europeans to come to South Africa were Portuguese explorers looking for a sea route to Asia.[1] In 1497, Vasco da Gama sailed round the Cape of Good Hope and became the first European explorer to reach India. For the next 150 years European sailors stopped periodically along the Cape to collect fresh water and repair battered ships. Soon it became a permanent provisioning post and the Dutch East India Company sent a group of settlers to establish a supply station. By 1657, a small number of these were released from their contracts to save the company money and were granted land to cultivate independently. These 'free burghers' and the others who soon joined them gradually moved northwards, out of the company's direct oversight.

Acute shortage of labour forced the company to import slaves from throughout the Dutch East Indian Empire, as well as from Madagascar, Angola and Mozambique. Slavery lasted nearly 180 years in South Africa, during which time racial distinctions became both more complicated (the descendants of the Asian slaves were among the people who later became known as 'coloured') and more stratified, as slave holding became a mark of wealth within the white community.

Peaceful relations between the settlers and the native inhabitants of the region did not last long. Open conflict broke out in which tens of thousands of natives were killed or imprisoned. Meanwhile, European immigrants, mostly Dutch, German and French Huguenot families arrived steadily, pushing up the white population. Those who moved into and around the northern reaches of the colony became known as Trekboers, due to their livelihoods as semi-nomadic farmers and ranchers. The name was later shortened to Boer, Dutch for 'farmer.'

By 1800, the white settler population had divided into two distinct groups. In rural areas slave-owning burghers, many of them poor and illiterate, had come to see themselves as a separate community, known as Boers or Afrikaaners. They spoke a variant of Dutch known as Afrikaans and cultivated a hostile relationship with their town-dwelling counterparts.

Great Britain seized control of the Cape Colony during the Napoleonic Wars, initially to protect its maritime trade with Asia. With the establishment of British rule in 1806, British lawmakers replaced the Dutch legislature in Cape Town, British style education replaced Dutch traditions of schooling and English became the official language. Many Boers did not welcome the increasing influence of British culture, nor the efforts to regulate the relations between the Boers and Africans. The most crippling blow to the Afrikaner way of life came when the British abolished slavery in 1834, which eliminated the primary source of labour for rural white farmers. Afrikaners responded with a mass northern exodus out of established colonial territory, and set up independent governments, first in Natal, then forming the Orange Free State and finally merging three smaller states into the South African Republic.

The British administration's tolerant attitude towards Afrikaner statehood changed dramatically with the discovery of diamonds in Kimberley and then gold in Witwatersrand, both Afrikaner held areas. Anglo-Boer tensions escalated and the four-year Boer War took a huge toll of lives, both white and black. The British emerged victorious and in 1910, the Afrikaner states joined the British states (Natal and the Cape) to form the Union of South Africa. The new government moved quickly to mend Anglo-Afrikaner differences by providing abundant loans and capital to all whites, made both Afrikans and English the official languages and allowed the formation of the Afrikaner National Party.

Africans were excluded from voting in three of the four colonies. But as the colony's mineral wealth become the source of an industrial revolution, the government's biggest challenge was to manage rapid urbanization while assuring supplies of cheap labour for both the mining industry and white farmers. By 1904, thousands and thousands of people had moved to cities like Johannesburg and Kimberley, seeking employment in the gold and diamond mines. This inevitably brought about increased contact between whites and Africans. The government's response was to impose strict policies of racial segregation. Africans, Coloureds (mixed-race people, usually of African, European and Asian descent) and Asians were confined to non-white slums, including Sophiatown, Alexandria and Orlando (present-day Soweto).

The South African government's discriminatory policies soon gave rise to protest groups. The South African Native Congress was the first black political organization, founded in 1898, which later expanded to create an even larger civil rights organization the SANNC, which became the African National Congress in 1923. Meanwhile labour protests multiplied, for the 'colour bar' excluded most non-whites from occupying skilled positions in the mines. The blacks in particular worked under extremely dangerous conditions at a fraction of the pay of white labourers. In addition to protests against the 'pass laws' (which restricted freedom of movement by requiring people to carry extensive documentation of their identity and employment at all times), there were organized boycotts of government run beer halls and bus lines. Thousands protested urban housing shortages by squatting on vacant land. By the end of the 1940s, uncontrollable urbanization and increasingly militant black resistance had convinced the colonial government that it needed more than racial segregation if it was to maintain both white rule and economic growth.

In 1948, the election of the Afrikaner-led National Party heralded a much more extreme policy, known as Apartheid. The term apartheid (from the Afrikaner word for 'apartness') has come to mean any legally sanctioned system of ethnic segregation. The first recorded use of the word is in 1917, during a speech by Jan Smuts, who became prime Minister of South Africa in 1919. The word was used as a political slogan of the National Party in the early 1940s. After the Afrikaner Nationalists came to power, the social custom of apartheid was systemized under law.

Apartheid pervaded South African culture as well as its laws. The "whites only" policy prohibited blacks from holding many jobs; they were not allowed to run businesses or professional practices in any areas designated for whites only. Police vans roamed the 'white area' to round up illegal blacks, i.e. those not carrying a pass. Schools, hospitals, beaches, trains, buses were segregated. Park benches were all labelled 'Europeans only'. There were no public swimming pools, libraries, parks, cinemas or any amenities except police stations in black areas. Cinemas in white areas, restaurants and hotels were not allowed to admit blacks except as workers. A white entering a shop would be served first ahead of blacks, already in the queue, irrespective of age, dress, or any other factors. Until the 1980s, blacks were always expected to step off the pavement to make way for any white pedestrian. A grown black man would be referred to as 'boy' to his face, by whites.

The implementation of the policy, later referred to as 'separate development' was made possible by the Population Registration Act of 1950, which put all South Africans into three racial categories: Bantu (black African), white, or Coloured (of mixed race). A fourth category (Indians and Pakistanis) was added later. The system of apartheid was enforced by a series of laws passed in the 1950s: the Group Areas Act of 1950 assigned races to different residential and business sections in urban areas, and the Land Acts of 1954 and 1955 restricted non-white residence to specific areas. These laws further restricted the already limited right of black Africans to own land, entrenching the white minority's control of over 80% of South African land. In addition, other laws prohibited most social contacts between the races; enforced the segregation of public facilities and separation of educational standards; created race-specific job categories; restricted the powers of non-white unions and curbed non-white participation in government.

Thus, apartheid sought to control and divide South African society through an elaborate set of race-based laws, restricting not only where people could live or work but also with whom they could marry or even associate. In addition to racial categories, apartheid recognized ten black African "tribes" or Bantu nations, each of which was assigned a rural Bantu homeland. Although the National Party claimed that these homelands allowed blacks to maintain their tribal customs and political structures, the primary objective of the homelands was to prevent formation of class-based resistance movements among black workers. In fact, intense poverty in the rural areas forced continued labour migration, which in turn led to growing tensions in the cities. In response the government passed increasingly restrictive policies: it banned inter-racial marriage in 1949 and declared black trade unions illegal in 1953.

Apartheid provided an ideological justification for massive ongoing population relocations. As black townships situated on the outskirts of major white urban cities became too large, the government tore them down and moved them farther out. The township of Sophiatown, for years the home of a thriving community of writers and artists was torn down, beginning in 1955. During apartheid's 44 year existence, thousands were forcibly relocated to areas with dwindling businesses and inefficient public services

In 1952, the ANC united with several coloured political groups to wage a non-violent campaign of boycotts, strikes and marches. In 1953, with the Bantu Education Act, the ruling Nationalist Party placed restrictions on the kind of education the blacks were entitled to. The anti-apartheid movement gained momentum in June 1955, when several groups gathered outside Johannesburg at a meeting known as the Congress of the People. Here a Freedom Charter outlining demands for a non-racial South Africa was adopted. Though the charter called for non-violent protests, the South African police responded to non-violent demonstrations by beatings, tortures and killings. In 1960, the police shot and killed 69 unarmed demonstrators in an anti-pass protest in the township of Sharpeville. All the victims were black. Most of them had been shot in the back.

The government banned the ANC and over the next few years continued with its policies of pass laws, relocations and other efforts of severe repression to suppress resistance. It declared a State of Emergency which lasted for 156 days, leaving 69 people dead and 187 wounded. The penalties imposed on political protest, even non-violent protest, were severe. During the states of emergency which continued intermittently until 1989, anyone could be detained without a hearing by a low-level police official for up to six months. Thousands died in custody, frequently after gruesome torture. Those who were tried were sentenced to death, banished or imprisoned for life, like Nelson Mandela. In response, the banned ANC along with the Communist Party together formed the guerilla army known as Umkhonto weSizwe, the "Spear of the Nation."

In the 1970s, political protest once again intensified, as even younger students participated. Student activists, among them the charismatic Steve Biko, promoted Black Consciousness, a philosophy of black pride and unity. In June 1976, elementary and secondary school students marched in protest of apartheid educational policies and police fired into the crowd. Several children were killed and many more injured; riots subsequently erupted in Soweto and throughout the country. The event provoked international condemnation and economic boycotts against South Africa.

Fearing complete administrative collapse. P.W. Botha and his government initiated new policies—such as granting Asian and Coloured, but not Africans, seats in parliament—in order to weaken anti-apartheid coalitions. At the same time it increased the size and presence of the police, army and intelligence forces. However, strikes, protests and demonstrations continued. The government declared a state of emergency and detained thousands of dissidents, harassed civic leaders, and censored the press.

But change was inevitable and in 1989, the National Party signalled its desire for a new approach when it replaced President Botha with the more moderate F.W. de Klerk. This was followed by the legalization of formerly banned black congresses and the release of imprisoned black leaders, including Nelson Mandela, who by then had spent 27 years behind bars. The release of Nelson Mandela was a watershed in the history of the fight against apartheid. The government came to realize that traditional ways of naked force and brutality were no longer a viable option. In 1994 the country's constitution was rewritten and free general elections were held for the first time in its history, and with Mandela as South Africa's first black president, the last vestiges of the apartheid system were finally outlawed.

NOTE

1. Excerpted in part from Kwame Anthony Appiah and Henry Louis Gates, Jr., ed., *The Encyclopaedia of the African and African American Experience* (A member of the Perseus Books Group, 1999), pp. 1756-61.

Literary Responses to Apartheid

The role of literature in a society is that of a mirror reflecting its politics, values and culture or challenging what it perceives as its evils. The system of apartheid was one of overwhelming oppressions. Hence it is not surprising that the literature being written at that time was a literature of protest.

Apartheid made itself felt in the way writers in South Africa responded to the social and political situation around them. Throughout the apartheid years, most writers were caught up in the culture of resistance. Black protest described the terrible conditions blacks lived in and suggested ways of overthrowing the government, while white protest dwelt on the guilt feelings of well-meaning, but powerless whites and tried to define what their role should be in a liberated black South Africa.

Andre Brink in his essay "Interrogating Silence" writes: "There was the need for black writers to articulate their oppression and this articulation passed through various clearly demarcated stages—a focus on the urban experience in the work of the *Drum* generation; an exploration of the parameters of oppression after Sharpeville; increasing exploration of literature as 'a tool in the struggle' after the Soweto uprisings of 1976; near triumphant affirmation during the several states of Emergency since 1986. White writers too, as more and more areas of reportage became proscribed by law, experienced the need 'to tell things as they are.' . . . The need to function as historian—that is, through 'reporting' and 'representing'—informed his/her activity and defined much of his/her scope."[1]

But because of strict censorship laws, very few writers, with the notable exception of Nadine Gordimer, survived long enough as writers to put out a sustained body of work. Gordimer's writing spans several different phases of apartheid: the rise to power of the National Party in 1948, The 1950 Immorality Amendment Act making 'carnal intercourse' between blacks and whites an offence, carrying a maximum penalty of seven years' imprisonment, which became the most tangible expression of the belief that the personal is the political, the turn to violence and armed struggle that was the aftermath of the Sharpeville massacre. In fact, the hidden wounds of apartheid, its unseen scars and silent scourge, are the real background and consequent force of Nadine Gordimer's fiction.

The interaction between the three dimensions of oppression in South Africa—those of race, class and of nationality—has led to a deep-seated colour prejudice, codified into an all-embracing racism, but this has always been resisted by a countervailing radicalism which specifically rejected colour and favoured a non-racial society. This is what leads Gordimer to call herself a "white African" and to say: "The tension between standing apart and being fully involved—that is what makes a writer, that is where we begin."[2]

An important writer of the Sixties and the Seventies was Alex La Guma and his work reflects the atmosphere of the times, from *A Walk in the Night* (1962) which reads like a catalogue of the evils of apartheid as a social system, the injustice of oppression and violence against which the characters are helpless, through *A Threefold Cord*, with its description of a township slum, to *The Stone Country* (1967) and *The Fog of the Season's End* (1972), both describing the brutality of prison life and then *Time of the Butcherbird* (1979), where the developing mood of resistance is accompanied by the development of political consciousness.

Speaking from the black point of view, Ndebele Njabulo writes: "we have seen the highly organized spectacle of the political wrestling match of the South African social formation. Everything in South Africa has been mind-bogglingly spectacular: the monstrous war machine developed over the years; the random massive pass raids; mass shootings and killings; mass economic exploitation, the ultimate symbol of which is the mining industry; the mass removals of the people; the spate of draconian laws passed with the spectacle of parliamentary promulgation, the luxurious life style of whites: servants, all-encompassing privilege, swimming pools and high commodity consumption; the sprawling monotony of architecture in African locations which are the very picture of poverty and oppression; the symbols are all over: the quintessence of obscene social exhibitionism. At the centre of it all, are the main actors: the aggressive Boer who has taken three centuries to develop the characteristics of the massive wrestler. It could be said, therefore, that the most outstanding feature of South African oppression is its brazen, exhibitionist openness."[3]

Njabulo further goes on to speak of the "absurdity" of daily life in South Africa, the triteness and barrenness of thought, which has resulted in an "emptying out of interiority" in writing. This led to the kind of writing that was known as 'protest' literature, which followed the disillusionment that came in the wake of the banning of the major political organizations. Creative writing became dramatically politicized with stories that revealed the spectacular ugliness of the South African situation in all its forms: the brutality of the Boer, the terrible farm and prison conditions, the phenomenal hypocrisy of the English-speaking liberal, the disillusionment of educated Africans, racial prejudice, the poverty of African life. The form was often autobiographical which allowed writers to show the dehumanizing aspects of apartheid through personal experience.

Nevertheless the very urgencies of the struggle against apartheid made it very difficult for writers to write about ordinary situations like a love relationship without direct political connotations, without inviting accusations of suppressing more 'urgent ' issues or of avoiding reality. One of the problems posed by the kind of literature produced in such circumstances was a tendency towards simple oppositions—us and them, black and white, good and bad.

There were writers, like Nadine Gordimer, for example, who recognized the dangers of reductivity where all complexities are reduced to a single, all-embracing formulation, and who argued for the critical importance of giving politics a natural place in fiction rather than simply propagandizing in fiction, of writing to expose the slew of contradictions that make up any life, not just a life shaped by racial discrimination.

This entails what Njabulo calls the necessity of rediscovering the ordinary He says: "the ordinary lives of people should be the direct focus of political interest because they constitute the very content of the struggle, for the struggle involves people, not abstractions. If it is a new society we seek to bring about in South Africa then that newness will be based on a direct concern with the way people actually live. That means a range of complex ethical issues involving man-man, man-woman, woman-woman, man-nature."[4]

NOTES

1. Andre Brink, "Interrogating Silence: new possibilities faced by South African literature," Derek Attridge and Rosemary Jolly, ed., *Writing South Africa: Literature, Apartheid and Democracy 1970-1995* (Cambridge University press, 1998).
2. *The Essential Gesture*, 1988.
3. Njabulo S. Ndebele, "Rediscovery of the Ordinary," *South African Literature and Culture* (Manchester University Press, 1994), pp. 41-42.
4. *Ibid.*, p. 57.

Nadine Gordimer on Apartheid and Writing

Gordimer, too, feels that her war against apartheid should be deeply implicit in all her writings, "since it is there." She says: "Although none of my books is formally political, the South African situation has conditioned me as a writer to an extent that could not have happened in any other country, through the extraordinary way in which the political situation has moulded the lives of the people around me. Not only the obvious confrontations of black and white are affected, whites among themselves are shaped by their peculiar position, just as black people are by theirs. I write about their private selves; often, even in the most private situations, they are what they are because their lives are regulated and their mores formed by the political situation. You see, in South Africa, society is the political situation. To paraphrase, one might say (too often), politics is character—in South Africa. I am not a politically minded person by nature. I don't suppose, if I had lived elsewhere, my writing would have reflected politics much, if at all. As it is, I have come to the abstractions of politics through the flesh and blood of individual behaviour. I didn't know what politics was about until I saw it all happening to people. If I've been influenced to recognize man as a political animal in my writing, then that's come about through living in South Africa."[1]

In an interview she once said "the real influence of politics on my writing is the influence of politics on people." Though she is quick to acknowledge that writers can't truly escape politics, still she champions the role of the imagination. She has said: "In my conduct and my action, I have submitted voluntarily and with self-respect to the discipline of the liberation movement. For my fiction, I have claimed and practiced my integrity to the free transformation of reality."[2]

In her essay "Three in a Bed: Fiction, Morals and Politics,"[3] she writes: "Not every fiction writer entering a relation with politics trades imagination for the hair shirt of the party hack. There is also the case of the writer whose imaginative powers are genuinely aroused by and involved with the spirit of politics as he or she personally experiences it. And it may not be the free choice of a Byron. It can be virtually inescapable in times and places of socially seismic upheaval. Society shakes, the walls of entities fall; the writer has known the evil, indifference, or cupidity of the old order and the spirit of creativity naturally pushes towards new growth. The writer is moved to fashion an expression of a new order, accepted on trust as an advance in human freedom that therefore also will be the release of a greater creativity."

Gordimer's views on writing are put forth in her Nobel Prize Banquet speech. She says: "Writing is, indeed, some kind of affliction in its demands as the most solitary and introspective of occupations. . . . We [writers] must live fully in order to secrete the substance of our work, but we have to work alone. From this paradoxical inner solitude our writing is what Roland Barthes called "the essential gesture" towards the people among whom we live, and to the world; it is the hand held out with the best we have to give. When I began to write as a very young person in a rigidly racist and uninhibited colonial society, I felt, as many others did, that I existed marginally on the edge of the world of ideas of imagination, of beauty. These taking shape in poetry and fiction, drama, painting and sculpture, were exclusive to that distant realm known as 'overseas'. It was the dream of my contemporaries, white and black, to venture there as the only way to enter the world of artists, It took the realization that the colour bar—I use that old, concrete image of racism—was like the gate of the law in Kafka's parable, which was closed to the supplicant throughout his life because he didn't understand that only he could open it. It took this to realize that what we had to do to find the world was to enter our own fully, first. We had to enter through the tragedy of our own particular place."[4]

In an interview to the *Boston Globe*, in October 1991, she said: "I have two roles in my life—one as a writer and another one, my commitment to the cause of freedom in South Africa and creating a new post-apartheid culture in South Africa."[5] Thus, her novels are anti-apartheid, not just because of her personal abhorrence of apartheid, but because the society which is the very stuff of her work is caught up in this horrific system.

NOTES

1. Qtd. James Vinson, ed., *Contemporary Novelists* (2nd ed., London: St. James Press, 1976), pp. 543-44.

2. Anthony Sampson, The *Observer* Review of Nadine Gordimer's *Living in Hope and History*, 1997.
3. Nadine Gordimer, *Living in Hope and History: Notes from our Century*.
4. Nadine Gordimer site on internet http://nobelprize.org/literature/laureates/1991/gordimer-speechhtml
5. http://www.boston.com/globe/search/stories/nobel/1991/1991jhtml

Nadine Gordimer's Works

Nadine Gordimer's first novel *The Lying Days* (1953) is a bildungsroman or a novel with characters in search of self-realization, charting a turbulent adolescent passage into wisdom and reconciliation and finding individual solutions to social problems. It is an account of the first 24 years in the life of its narrator Helen Shaw, as she gropes blindly into the adult world of love, responsibility and human commitment—a somewhat disguised Nadine Gordimer growing up in Springs. It describes the search for satisfactory personal relationships in which differences of class and colour will be forgotten.

The novel traces the development of the protagonist from small mining town girl to member of the bohemian Johannesburg set as she lives through the turmoil of the early days of the Nationalist Party rule and the onslaught of apartheid. Helen moves away in search of her own identity, from the narrow confines of her sheltered existence in the white community of officials working for a mining company, the three phases of her life signified by the three sections of the novel—The Mine, The Sea, The City. In the first part, Helen inhabits a world effectively sheltered from the world of the black natives that forms its periphery, the "filthy kaffir stores" where one could "breathe in heaven knows what dirt and disease my mother condemned."[1] This racist mentality is so deeply ingrained in and unconsciously absorbed by the child, that it makes her regard this other world as alien, arousing in her both curiosity and fear, and blurring the edges of reality so that there is no distinction between the serious and the trivial—the suffering that leads to a strike of mine workers becomes something with which she cannot connect: "Those native boys sitting about making a noise the way they liked to in the garden, and the lovely tea all ready in Mrs. Ockert's beautiful lounge. . . . That couldn't be a strike." (39)

The visit to the Kochs by the 17 year-old Helen and Helen's relationship with Ludi Koch marks the second stage of her development. It is not merely a sexual awakening that she experiences, it is an awakening to the truth of her situation. When Ludi speaks of "That life on the Mine is the narrowest, most mechanical unrewarding existence you could think of in any nightmare" (56), it is a perspective that has not occurred to her so far. It is thus a movement away from the claustrophobic white enclave towards a wider world where the "real flow of life" goes on.

This growth of awareness is given a political focus in the third section by Helen's friendship with Mary Seswayo at the University. The fact that there are no public toilet facilities for blacks in the Johannesburg shopping centre, brings her face to face with the question of human dignity. Finally it is her mother's horrified reaction when she invites Mary to stay with her—even though she makes arrangements for her to be put up in the "cooler," a storeroom originally built for keeping food and which would be "neither inside the house or out in the yard with Anna [the maid], but something in between" (187)—that lifts her out of her self-absorption into an attempt to experience the reality of others. But the initial courage and curiosity that permit Helen early in the novel to venture outside the mine compound and into university life are insufficient to equip her to challenge meaningfully the social expectations of her world. Though she becomes involved, tentatively, fearfully in a protest (an actual historical event, on May Day, 1950) against the Suppression of Communism Act and witnesses the shooting of a black protester, she is not sufficiently empowered to take action. She remains a spectator rather than an actor. Thus failure in personal relationships is paralleled by failure of political consciousness. Nevertheless, there is an incipient optimism, the "phoenix illusion" as Gordimer calls it, hope for a future in which the aspirations of all will be secure.

The early novels chart the dilemmas associated with the race question which is so systematically and deliberately woven into all aspects of South African life and culture that liberal humanism and fundamental good will fail in its wake. They also chronicle a growing disillusion with liberalism as a creed to combat apartheid. In *A World of Strangers* (1958) and later *Occasion for Loving* (1963), which brilliantly capture the mood of politically volatile Johannesburg at the time, even promising relations among black and white intellectuals and artists founder on the massive inequities established by the police state.

In *A World of Strangers* (1958), Gordimer's second novel, the narrator is a young upper middle class Englishman Toby Hood, who comes to South Africa on an assignment for his family's publishing house. He is faced with a choice between the obvious appeals of an opulent white society and the harsher path of commitment to the cause of black nationalism His superficial, elegant mistress, Cecil

Rowe is part of high white society which surrounds itself with the privileges of position and power, effectively cocooning itself from the wretchedness and misery that is the lot of the black population. She belongs to a class whose feelings have atrophied into what Gordimer calls elsewhere a "moral sclerosis." In contrast is another woman who is committed to political action out of personal conviction, Anna Louw, the Afrikaner activist, who introduces Toby Hood to a world of people who are engaged in the struggle for black political emancipation, chiefly Steven Sitole. As an outsider, Toby is able to exist in both worlds. This breaks Toby's languid detachment. But he is equally ineffective in both worlds. He is unable to influence Cecil out of her acceptance of racial superiority and loses her to a conventional marriage in the comfortable world of white privilege and he loses Steven to death in a police raid. While Steven's death jolts Toby into acknowledging the racist horrors of the South African regime, he can do nothing to bridge the divide between the world of strangers and the novel ends with his opting out to return to the mother country

The existence in the late fifties of an interracial social and cultural group in Johannesburg became the site for an optimism which saw serious commitment to another person across the colour bar as a possible solution to the evils of racial discrimination. But very soon, Sharpeville and the banning of the ANC and the PAC put an end to this optimism.

Gordimer's third novel, *Occasion for Loving* (1963), reflects this uncertainty. It was published after Sharpeville, when opposition movements which had hitherto advocated passive resistance and non-violence were driven to embrace violence as the only way in which they could achieve their ends. The 1950 Immorality Amendment Act making 'carnal intercourse' between blacks and whites an offence, carrying a maximum penalty of seven years of imprisonment provided Nadine Gordimer an opportunity to once again explore the impact of apartheid on personal lives, choices and possibilities. Racially motivated state violence makes the idea of multi-racial cooperation naïve; it now necessitates the pursuit of black freedom by blacks for blacks. Gordimer's novel charts the failure of cross-racial personal contacts and the dilemma of the white South African liberal.

Jessie and Tom Stilwell invite their friend Boaz Davis, who is researching African music and his wife Ann to stay with them. Ann develops a tempestuous love affair with Gideon Shibalo, a black artist who has had to forfeit a scholarship because his application for a passport has been rejected by the government. The relationship of the black Gideon Sibalo with three white women provides a context for an examination of differing responses to the question of apartheid. For Jessie Stilwell who believes "The whole way we live becomes a political gesture above everything else" the sense of connection is intuitive. She sees in him her own struggle to maintain a balance in the face of loneliness, unhappiness and frustration. Ann's feelings about the injustice of the colour bar are merely part of the ethos of the period in which she had grown up, it is not deeply felt; and this makes her unprepared for the harsh realities she encounters as a white companion to a black man. There is an element of egoism in her love for Gideon "the black man that everyone pushed away and that she, she had put her hand out and touched"[2] and an attitude of role-playing that cannot withstand the pressures. Ironically, even a selfless devotion like that of Callie Stow's, a Scotswoman who leads a rich life of her own as activist, social worker and intellectual, and who opens her heart to Gideon, thinking nothing of darning his socks and waiting for him in a public street corner, is doomed, for Gideon's male ego chafes under her imposed code of "self respect"—"He did not feel like her lover." (123) In a tortured world, neither love nor passion can survive. All feelings become ambivalent. Gideon feels a kind of pride in possessing a beautiful white woman like Ann, with her thin wrists and ankles and careless style contrasting with the thick calves and plastic smartness of the township girls, but in his heart he knows that the one place that has warmth and truth is the black township where there was no shade of ambiguity and all were committed to the struggle.

Ann, too, sees only one part of the African world, its warmth, zest and freshness but does not see the uncertainty and pain behind it. And so when she comes face to face with the harsh realities of life with a black companion—that she cannot walk casually into a hotel and soak in a hot bath as she had done earlier or even have coffee in the petrol station's tea room, because Gideon will not be allowed in, she leaves him.

For Jessie who is only too willing to reach across and connect, the fact of being white becomes an insurmountable hurdle. "They believed in the integrity of personal relations against the distortions of laws and society. What stronger and more proudly personal bond was there than love? Yet even between lovers they had seen blackness count, the personal return inevitably to the social, the private to the political. There was no recess of being, no emotion so private that white privilege did not single you out there; it was a silver spoon clamped between your jaws and you might choke on it for all the chance there was of dislodging it. So long as the law remains unchanged, nothing could bring integrity to personal relationships." (279)

Gordimer's next novel was *The Late Bourgeois World* (1966) which, she said in an interview, "shows the breakdown of my belief in the liberal ideas."[3] It was also "an attempt to look into the specific character of the social climate that produced the wave of young white saboteurs in 1963-64."[4] It takes as its starting point the political trials of 1964 in which a number of white intellectuals were found guilty of sabotage. The background to this novel was provided by the activities of the African Resistance Movement (consisting predominantly of white students and young professionals) a group which played a part in the series of bombings of post offices and other strategic targets, together with the militant wings of the ANC and the PAC. The mood is sombre as doubts and uncertainties about the possibilities of political progress surface.

Examining the case of one such would be revolutionary, in the context of his family, his friends and his political associates, Nadine Gordimer evokes with considerable power the sterility and fear which increasingly make the "bourgeois" world of the middle class whites irrelevant and in a metaphorical sense dead.

The two epigraphs illuminate the themes of the novel: "There are possibilities for me, certainly; but under what stone do they lie?"—Franz Kafka and "The madness of the brave is the wisdom of life"—Maxim Gorky. Kafka's question finds new urgency in the novel. One Saturday morning, Elizabeth Van Den Sandt opens a telegram telling her that her ex-husband Max, has drowned himself. Much has gone down into the sea with him. They had wanted to live well, in the true sense, like human beings, not at the cost of oppressing others, but that is not what South African white society allows them to do. Max is highly strung, intelligent and he rejects the kind of life where anything outside the smug maintenance of white power and respectability is seen as treason. The blinkered attitude of his parents drives Max to rebel: "when Mrs. Van Den Sandt spoke of 'we South Africans' she meant the Afrikaans and English speaking white people and when Theo Van Den Sandt called for a 'united South Africa going forward to an era of progress and prosperity for all' he meant the unity of the same two white groups and higher wages and bigger cars for them. For the rest—the ten or eleven million 'natives'—their labour was directed by various Acts of no interest outside Parliament, and their lives were incidental to their labour, since until the white man came they knew nothing better than a mud hut in the veld."[5] Max's parents represent the 'decent' white society which is unaffected by the home-made bombs, the riots, the marches, the shootings and deplores the inhumanity of violence and "reserving the right of constitutional action to themselves alone, commend it to others as the only decent way to achieve change—should one want such a thing." (43)

Max's personality is distorted by inability to find acceptance or admiration anywhere, despite his high ideals and his genuine desire to help the cause of the black people. In his restlessness, he joins one political organization after another, but finds himself increasingly alienated by both the white society which disapproves of him and the blacks. He experiences the "isolation of his colour" (81) and his emotional instability leads him to betray his colleagues during police interrogation. He expiates his guilt, according to his own code of honour, by driving his car into the sea. It is an action that is "the madness of the brave," even though ultimately futile. Max's search for "possibilities" fails, but Elizabeth feels impelled to carry on his cause by allying herself with the black activist Luke Fokase and offering her help as conduit for money for the resistance movement, even though she is unsure of what this will mean for her. But at least she will not be "dead" as the other whites. The last line points to this commitment: "The slow even beats of my heart repeats me, like a clock, afraid, alive, afraid, alive, afraid, alive." (160)

In the late 1960s, Nadine Gordimer travelled a great deal through the new nations of Africa, lecturing on African literature. This experience bore fruit in the shape of her next novel, *The Guest of Honour* (1971) in which she once again examines the role of the whites in the black liberation movement. The honoured guest is James Bray, who is invited to attend the independence celebrations of a newly independent African state, headed by the leaders Adamson Mweta and Edward Shinza. Bray had earlier been expelled from the country, when the whites had petitioned the Colonial Office to have Bray removed for supporting the black nationalists. Back in the district he had once ruled, he is at first optimistic for the new country, then disquieted by rumours of corruption and police state methods especially the violent torture and interrogation of a young worker from the fish factory for ostensibly instigating other workers. Although there is little he can do to avert the strife which neo-colonial tensions make inevitable or even to create a better educational system, he nevertheless knows that what he does is right and necessary. As he witnesses the factionalism and violence that erupt as revolutionary ideals are subverted by ambition and greed, Bray is forced to choose between loyalty to his old friends in the government and blind faith in a revolutionary future—a choice that becomes both his triumph and his undoing

The novel has two epigraphs: Turgenev's "An honourable man will end by not knowing where to live," and Ernesto Che Guevara's "Many will call me an adventurer—and that I am, only one of a different sort—one of those who risks his skin to prove his platitudes." These quotations point to the twin concepts of honour and bravery that govern the existence of those whites in Africa who are not conditioned by the attitudes of racism. As Naidu explicates: "Although he is Mweta's guest, he becomes increasingly involved in the destructive factionalism within the emerging nation when he learns of Shinza's allegiance to the rural population and the exploited workers of the mining and fishing industries. Eventually, as he is leaving the country to procure arms for Shinza, he is mistakenly ambushed and killed by Shinza supporters. Like Max and Liz Van Den Sandt, Bray has an authentic recognition of the moral imperatives guiding his presence in Africa. Bray chooses to act on these imperatives with integrity. Nevertheless,

Gordimer warns her readers that liberal idealism, although well-intended, is fraught with peril and personal sacrifice."[6]

Bray's relationship with the South African girl, Rebecca, is in some way a relationship of kindred spirits who live "not as an adversary but a participant."[7] Though Bray tries to assert the values he feels as permanent against a background of bewilderment and instability, he fails to bring about any significant change and is killed by the very people he has tried to help. His failure however has the redeeming quality of truthfulness. The last lines of the novel, spoken by Emmanuelle who represents the "white" viewpoint, highlights the tragic irony of his situation: "These nice white liberals getting mixed up in things they don't understand. What did he expect?"

Gordimer's sixth novel *The Conservationist* (1974) was the joint winner of the Booker Prize in 1974. The protagonist is Mehring, the pig-iron tycoon, at the heart of the international trade in raw materials. He represents the white person who negotiates his African environment as a white man first and as an African second. His wealth has limited his vision of the world and the epithet "conservationist" establishes with cutting irony the hollowness of his relationship to the land. The farm is his property in the sense that the whole country is property to the white man. In acquiring it, he sees it as a good investment, a way to minimize tax losses and also as a safe place to take a woman, and his conviction that only a productive farm can be beautiful is wholly mercenary. The farm gives him a heady sense of power and status, and the black farm hands like Jacobus and Solomon, who are the ones who look after the land, exist in his perception only as a convenience. Dominance and control govern his attitudes, and his self-centredness and isolation is highlighted by the quotations from Zulu mythology derived from Henry Callaway's *The Religious System of the Amazulu*, where the relationship of man with the earth is seen as sacred and as a source of communal sharing and celebration: "I pray for corn that many people may come to this village of yours and make a noise and glorify you" and "I ask also for children that this village may have a large population and that your name may never come to an end." Mehring's distance from the culture of the land that he inhabits and his materialism is evidenced in his casual attitude to the kaffir rain queen—a doll used for magical purposes. Its deep-rooted symbolic significance eludes Mehring, who sees it as an object to make money: "Museums in America pay fortunes these days to get hold of these things."

Mehring is not only an exploiter but a sexual predator as well. He indulges in frequent erotic imaginings about young girls and women, and the scene in which he surreptitiously violates the body of the young girl in the seat next to him on the plane, reveals his "sexual fascism." For him the "extreme intimacy" is also "the extreme of detachment."[8] This arrogance leads him to pick up a female hitchhiker and then to abandon her when there is a threat to his own safety. He does not care whether she is raped or robbed, because as he says callously, "coloured or poor-white, whichever she is, their brothers or fathers take their virginity good and early."

The focus of the narrative is the discovery of a dead body of a black man on the farm. Though the police give it a hasty, improper burial, it becomes an actual, "living" part of the land, becoming a disruptive presence in Mehring's consciousness. The paradox is that the man who owns the land because he has paid for it can never be a part of the land, because he does not belong to it. The dead man is associated in Mehring's mind with a past with which he can never connect: "Come to think of it, all the earth is a graveyard, you never know when you're walking over heads—particularly this continent, this cradle of man, prehistoric bones and the bits of shaped stone . . . that were weapons and utensils." (141) The dead man lives on in nature: "Already the reeds must be eight inches high."

Thus in the end when a storm blows up and unearths the body, it's powerful, destructive, but cleansing symbolism represents the inevitability of African resurgence. This recognition precipitates a psychological crisis which drives Mehring from the farm. It is a kind of poetic justice that he meets his death, not in earth, but among the cyanide-rich mine dumps, the ugly by-product of industrialization and which had earlier led him to erotic arousal.

David Ward points out: "*The Conservationist* shares with *The Waste Land* its underlying structure of an arid and dispossessed land being restored to life by the return of the rain, the life giving properties of the burial of the dead and death by water." (141) The last lines of the novel, in which the body is finally given a burial by the farm people, emphasise this renewal: "The one whom the farm received had no name. He had no family but their women wept a little for him. There was no child of his present but their children were there to live after him. They had put him away to rest, at last, he had come back. He took possession of this earth, theirs; one of them." (252)

Nadine Gordimer's work has consistently responded to the history of her country, and with the publication of *Burger's Daughter* in 1979, she spans action ranging from the 50s through the repressive 60s to the Black Consciousness movement of the mid-70s with the Soweto uprising occurring towards the end. Once again, she introduces a demand for action and commitment into her analysis of the complexities of white involvement in apartheid politics.

In *Burger's Daughter*, she examines the ethical dilemmas and choices that confront those who are born into the tradition of white political resistance. Rosa is the daughter of prominent white activists, Lionel and Cathy Burger, both of whom suffer imprisonment and who have dedicated their whole lives to the cause of freedom and justice for the oppressed. Rosa, being their daughter is shaped by an ideal of service and self-sacrifice. The narrative unfolds through Rosa's unspoken conversations with three auditors—Conrad, her ex-lover, who shows Rosa how much she has suppressed her emotional needs out of loyalty to the cause her family supports; Katya, Lionel's ex-wife who has retired from active politics into a pleasant self-indulgent life in southern France; and in the third section, Lionel Burger himself as Rosa returns to be jailed in the very prison where he served his sentence. Though Rosa cannot escape her inheritance, she feels the need to assess and define for herself what the commitment means for her personally. It may have led her to emotional repression and Rosa recalls the torment she had undergone psychologically over the visits she was required to make to the political prisoner Noel de Witt posing as his fiancee, a relationship in which her adolescent infatuation for him can find no expression.

Her conflicting feelings with regard to her heritage is brought to a head in the scene in which Rosa watches helplessly as a black man beats a donkey. This produces in her a sense of revulsion, for to intervene would mean asserting her "white" authority. The episode is also an intimation of the deep structure of violence which guarantees her white authority. It is a traumatic moment of bitter disillusionment. Her feeling of acute marginalization prompts her to withdraw from radical political activity and move to Europe. In her relationship with the married Bernard Chabalier, she experiences a brief interlude of intense personal fulfillment, but she soon realizes it for what it is—an irresponsible escapism

The turning point comes when she suddenly receives a phone call from Bassie (little boss), the black boy who had been brought up with her almost like a brother. She is shocked at his furious repudiation of his pet name, and for the first time, she comes to know what his real name is—Zwezinlima ("suffering land"). The fact that her family's well-meant attempts at racial integration had merely served to suppress an individual identity, and that her acceptance of accolade as Lionel Burger's daughter could be interpreted as complicity in the system of privilege and oppression, shakes her. Along with her friendship with Marisa Kgosana, wife of an imprisoned political leader, whose sensual perfection combined with keen intellect suggests a rounded political ideal, this leads her to a different perspective about the nature of her commitment to the revolutionary tradition in the context of the emerging Black Consciousness movement in the post-Soweto reality. She is impelled to return to her family's heritage of political activism and the implication is that for all liberal whites, a reassessment of their role in the anti-apartheid struggle is needed.

The condition of white South Africans in a new political order of an imaginary future becomes the theme of Gordimer's next novel, *July's People* (1981). It is an apocalyptic story of a terrifying interregnum, in which a white couple, Bam and Maureen Smales, with their children flee a revolution which deprives them of their power and status and take refuge in the village of their black servant, whom they call July. The epigraph, from Antonio Gramsci's *Prison Notebooks*—"The old is dying and the new cannot be born in this interregnum there arises a great diversity of morbid symptoms"—points to the traumatic anxiety, uncertainty, helplessness and loss of identity that the central characters experience.

The Smales are caught between the opposite polarities of a life governed by 'white' codes and another kind of existence where these codes have little meaning. Their liberalism has been a pretence, more a matter of protecting their own selves than a genuine reaching out and is doomed to failure. "They joined political parties and 'contact groups in willingness to slough privilege it was supposed to be their white dog nature to guard with Mirages and tanks; they were not believed. They had thought of leaving. . . . They had stayed; and told each other and everyone else that this and nowhere else was home, while knowing, as time left went by, the reason had become they couldn't get their money out."[9]

Their complacence and arrogance is thinly disguised as benevolent generosity. To Maureen, July is just "the boy" for the house, "decently paid, clothed by them in two sets of uniform, given Wednesdays and alternate Sundays free, allowed to have his friends visit him," and yet she knows that she indulged him only because she had been afraid to lose him and the comforts he provided. "He must have known, when she handed some new object on to him, it was because it was shoddy or ugly to her, and if it were some old object, it was because she no longer valued it." (67) His dignity as a man is of no importance to her.

It is therefore a reversal of roles that July now is the one in whose hands their lives are held. Their total dependency on him now replicates his earlier subservience to them, in which he had to ask for everything. "An aspirin. Can I use the telephone? Nothing in that house was his." (155) Now Maureen realizes "She was already not what she was. No fiction could compete with what she was finding she did not know. . . . They had nothing." (29)

As refugees in July's village, they are forced back into an existence which nullifies the importance of personal achievements and material possessions. Stripped of all the trappings of power they experience a chilling loss of sense of self. "Us and them. Who is us, now and who them?" (117)

They discover hitherto unknown aspects of themselves—Bam, that he is a killer, Maureen, that she has indulged in sadism and theft. As the novel ends, Maureen is seen running towards the helicopter that circles overhead, "like a solitary animal . . . the enemy of all that would make claims of responsibility," (160) a final exposure of the emptiness and bankruptcy of the values epitomized by the Smales.

Gordimer's next novel *A Sport of Nature* (1987) uses as an epigraph the OED definition of a "sport of nature" as "a departure from the parent stock or type," a "spontaneous mutation" or "new variety." In the character of Hillela, Gordimer explores the relationship between sexuality and political action. Hillela is involved with black men as partner in the same cause, but Gordimer views with progressive disillusionment the attempts to bridge the gulf between black and white that shapes the nature of these relationships. Hillela's first husband Whaila, a black revolutionary, is assassinated, and her later union with the African rebel general Reuel is presented in an ambivalent light, as a celebration of the possibility of racial integration but at the same time viewed with ironical clarity as an unattainable Utopia. Yet the attempts signify a kind of heroism in its search for an emerging identity that is valid in its own way.

Nadine Gordimer's next novel *My Son's Story* (1990) is about a coloured family ravaged by the father's affair with a white human rights advocate. It is the story of a man's evolution as a political activist and the toll it takes on his family and on him. It is also a picture of a marriage and an extra-marital affair set against the backdrop of segregated South Africa, even as the winds of change begin to blow. Sonny is an exemplary husband and father, the pride of his community which leads him to a role as leader in the revolutionary cause. Meeting Hannah, who is a representative of a human rights organization, he is swept into an affair that leads to the breakup of his family. The tragic end of his high hopes and ideals are partially narrated by his teenaged son Will, bitter and cynical over his father's betrayal. The interplay of public and private realities reveals the agonizing moral complexities which relationships bring in a world that divides human beings. As *The New York Times* review noted, Gordimer herself said about this book: "The book is really about the problems the ordinary forms of love bring within a particular context, in which love of country is inextricably bound up with these other types of love. And by love of country, I don't mean gung-ho patriotism, but involvement with the time."

A sense of disillusionment, undercut though it is by a brave hopefulness, characterizes Gordimer's next novel, *None to Accompany Me* (1994). The repression of apartheid and the delusions of the colour bar, long the leit motifs of her work, are dead. Yet in the new world that is emerging there is turmoil as old relational patterns are turned upside down. Set in the turbulent period before the first non-racial elections and the beginning of majority rule in South Africa, Gordimer shows Vera Stark, her protagonist, moving out of the tangle of personal relationships with husband, children and friends, to a complete involvement with public life "group thinking, group decisions" as a lawyer fighting for the blacks who have been dispossessed of their lands, "not out of the white guilt people talked about, but out of a need to take up . . . the time and place, to which, by birth, she understood she had no choice but to belong."[10] Though there has been an initial sense of euphoria—"No more police, no more dogs, no more tear-gas, no more beatings on the way to the Black Maria"—it soon fades away as the reality of squatter camps of jagged tin and tattered plastic sheets becomes evident and poverty and violence continue. Vera feels the "very inappropriateness of any personal preoccupation arising from a situation where all individuality was in dissolution in terror and despair." (121) For a while she finds reassurance and a certain tranquillity in her relationship with Zeph Rapulana, the black people's representative with whom she comes into contact in the course of her work, but she is shaken to find the human distance between his blackness and her whiteness unbridgeable. The epigraphs that Gordimer uses aptly define her situation: "We must never be afraid to go too far, for truth lies beyond"—Marcel Proust, and "None to accompany me on this path: Nightfall in Autumn"—Basho (17th century Japanese poet).

The House Gun (1998) is Nadine Gordimer's 12th novel and is set in post-apartheid South Africa. Harald and Claudia Lingard are like the whites in most of Gordimer's novels, passively liberal and ostensibly unprejudiced. Their safe and comfortable world is shaken when they find out that their son, Duncan, has been arrested for killing one of his housemates. His guilt is undeniable, for he has confessed to the crime. Suddenly, the shadow of violence, which uptil now had belonged to the other world and from which they had felt themselves to be insulated, falls on their complacent lives. They are jolted out of their oblivion to a recognition of the bloody history of their nation where crime has spiralled so sharply that guns are kept for protection in almost every household. The novel records the psychological impact of this incident on the parents as they search for the truth and their coming face to face with their hitherto unacknowledged prejudices as they put their faith in Hamilton Motsamai, the black lawyer Duncan has hired to defend him.

Gordimer's latest novel is *The Pick-Up* (2001), an exploration of freedom, responsibility, love and identity. In an unnamed country that clearly is South Africa, the heroine, Julie Summers, rejects the materialism of her affluent, privileged background and falls for a dark-skinned foreigner who has repaired her car. Julie finds Abdu different from the circle of intellectuals and free-thinkers to which she belongs and whose meeting place is a café called 'The Table.' Julie and Abdu become lovers, and we learn that he is an illegal immigrant who works as a mechanic because that is the only kind of work available to him. The relationship between the two is complex, chiefly because Julie through it seeks to reject the privileged life style that Abdu, through this same relationship, seeks to attain. When Abdu is deported, Julie accompanies him to his exile. But the desert country that is Abdu's home and which he had sought to leave, becomes for Julie a real home where relationships are deep and caring. She feels something that she has never felt before. Now Abdu is known by his real name Ibrahim ibn Musa. Ibrahim does not reciprocate Julie's views; he thinks her feelings for his people are just another passing fancy. He leaves for America, while Julie stays behind. The novel leaves behind many unanswered questions—who is more open-minded, freer, more faithful to the true self. The gap between individuals and cultures is not easily bridged.

Nadine Gordimer has several volumes of short stories to her credit and it is a form of which she is a master. They are *Face to Face* (1949), *The Soft Voice of the Serpent and Other Stories* (1950), *Six Feet of Country* (1956), *Friday's Footprint and Other Stories* (1960), *Not for Publication and Other Stories* (1965), *Livingstone's Companions*

(1971), *Some Monday for Sure* (1976), *Town and Country Lovers* (1980), *A Soldier's Embrace* (1980), *Something Out There* (1984), *Jump and Other Stories* (1991), *Crimes of Conscience* (1991), *Loot and Other Stories* (2003). Her stories often use themes similar to those of her novels, portraying individuals who struggle to avoid, confront, or change the conditions under which they live. Some depict ordinary people defying apartheid in their daily lives or show how apartheid insulates the daily lives of ordinary blacks and whites. Others offer ironic overviews of South African society. Still others explore the temperaments of individuals who unwittingly support the mechanisms of racial separation.

Gordimer's body of work includes several pieces on literary criticism and essays on contemporary culture and society. They include *African Literature: The 1972 lectures at the University of Cape Town*, *On the Mines* (1973) *What Happened to Burger's Daughter or, How South African Censorship Works* (1980), *Lifetimes under Apartheid* (1986), *The Essential Gesture: Writing, Politics and Places* (1988), *Writing and Being* (1995) and *Living in Hope and History: Notes from Our Century* (1999).

NOTES

1. Nadine Gordimer, *The Lying Days* (Jonathan Cape, 1953), p. 18.
2. Nadine Gordimer, *Occasion for Loving* (Penguin, 1964), p. 152.
3. Dominic Head, *Nadine Gordimer* (Cambridge University Press, 1994), p. 77.

4. David Ward, *Chronicles of Darkness* (Routledge, 1989), p. 119.
5. Nadine Gordimer, *The Late Bourgeois World* (Jonathan Cape, 1966), p. 40.
6. Pushpa Naidu Parekh and Siga Fatima Jagne, ed., *Post Colonial African Writers: A Bio-Bibliographical Critical Sourcebook* (Fitzroy Dearborn, 1998), p. 191.
7. Nadine Gordimer, *A Guest of Honour* (Penguin, 1970), p. 519.
8. Nadine Gordimer, *The Conservationist* (Jonathan Cape, 1974), p. 124.
9. Nadine Gordimer, *July's People* (Penguin, 1981), p. 8.
10. Nadine Gordimer, *None to Accompany Me* (Penguin, 1994), p. 121.

My Son's Story: The Characters

Sonny

The central character of the novel is Sonny, whose story told by Will, his son and the author of the book, this is. He belongs to ordinary folk, his great-grandfather probably coming from the diamond diggings in Kimberley, a photograph showing him among a work gang holding sieves used in panning for alluvial diamonds. Sonny's own father sets up trade in a garage as an upholsterer. However, it is Sonny who leaves earth, cement, wood and kapok behind and takes up pen and book, becoming the first in his family to complete the full years of schooling and become a teacher. He is the pride of his family and of his community. Their pride was not only the rejoicing in claiming one who has moved up out of their class, but that pride came from an instinct for Sonny's distinction. Though Sonny was dark skinned, something that normally might have downgraded him among them, in his case it was accompanied by deep eyes and hands that were alert, yet bestowed calm when resting in a handshake or a caress. "Everything he was and did evidenced distinction."[1] (3) And when Sonny marries Aila, she has that same distinction which arouses his "particular unspoken respect for her."

Both Sonny and Aila feel that the true meaning of life was in living useful lives, something that had to do with responsibility to the community. For Sonny, this translates into a special accountability for the welfare of the children at school. A lover of Shakespeare, whose works, in a cheap complete edition he reads and re-reads with devotion, he now buys books to grasp theories of the school's function in social education. His book-case has not only Marx, Lenin, Fanon, Gandhi and Nkrumah, Mandela and Biko, but also Kafka and D.H. Lawrence. He starts a parent-teacher association, collects money for special equipment for handicapped children, takes groups of senior boys and girls to do repairs in the yard rooms of pensioners. He enterprisingly approaches the Rotary and Lions Clubs to send doctors, lawyers and members of theatre groups and music groups to lecture or perform in the school hall.

Self-respect is Sonny's religion and that is what he teaches his children—do what will enable you to keep your self-respect. This credo leads Sonny through the path of contemplative privacy to public activity, imprisonment and trial. Along with the desire to be useful is his desire for self-improvement. He feels that he could improve the quality of life for the school, for the community if he himself 'enriched his mind' Though he is denied many avenues like forums for political debate, theatre, the music society, the bird watcher's group or even the library, he enrolls in a correspondence course in comparative literature. This leads him to understand Kafka, whose writings become meaningful in the context of Sonny's own life and the society around him: "The sin for which the schoolteacher's kind were banished to a prescribed area, proscribed in everything they did, procreating, being born, dying, at work or at play, was the sin Joseph K. was summoned to answer for to an immanent power, not knowing what the charge was, knowing only that if that power said he was guilty of something, then he was decreed so." (10-11) But he does not believe with Kafka "that the power in which people are held powerless exists only in their own submission. He knew better."

Because Sonny had managed to extricate himself from the "bewilderment" of debt, ignorance, promiscuity and insecurity that crushed his people, they looked up to him as one of their own, powerless like them, who yet had a special kind of self-respect; and who took up a responsibility for their lives in a different way from that of their masters. "He did things for other people the way he did for us—his family. That was it; to give came to him naturally, as it came to them to take."

Sonny is an exemplary father and husband, keeping everything in the house in good order and teaching Will how to change fuses, replace the cord on the steam iron and to play chess. Though he did not hide from the children the fact that there were many places they couldn't go, many things they couldn't do, he still managed to build up a "charmed circle" round their lives.

Sonny was clear about his chosen path—he would better himself by studying for a higher qualification, not by going to meetings or getting arrested on a march; and so his concern with the demand that was being raised for equality among the black was only a passing concern for him, chiefly because he was so preoccupied with an inner life that he took little notice of the humiliations and slights that pushed at him the moment he ventured outside the community. Though he read the newspapers and followed the political trials, though he was aware of an instinct of responsibility that extended outwards, initially he limits it to participation of his family in community projects.

But when the children start keeping out of class and carrying slogans written on cardboard, Sonny faces a challenge. He shows his solidarity with the children's cause by joining them, correcting the words spelt wrong on the placards, and finally persuading the principal to let him go with them when they decide to march across the veldt to show solidarity with the children who had been locked out of school by the police. He manages for some time to keep them peaceful, but he is unable to keep petrol and matches out of their hands. Searching for the children who have been arrested, Sonny goes to the police station and his name enters police records. The principal buckles under pressure and dismisses Sonny, but his authority wavers before this particular member of his staff.

A new phase opens in Sonny's life when he is approached to form a local committee; he is elected to the regional executive and he starts making speeches. He has the advantage of his name, which implied approachability and closeness to the people he would address, and he excels as a speaker. Now his profession becomes the meetings, the speeches, the campaigns, the delegations to the authorities.

When Sonny decides to move in to live among whites as part of the campaign against segregation, he has the strength of his mission to arm him, but for Aila it is an uprooting of her ordered and disciplined life. Inevitably, Sonny's political involvement, promotion of boycotts and participation in illegal gatherings, leads to his imprisonment. He is allowed to see only Aila and once or twice, the children, and during these visits Aila, beautifully groomed as usual, talks to him about family matters, reassuring him that everything was all right. But the silences between them that were so comfortable at home, now become a real silence without communication. When she writes to him, the regulation five hundred words are all about family matters.

Sonny is thus entirely unprepared for the visit of Hannah who is monitoring for a human rights organization. Unlike Aila, she manages to use an abstract vocabulary in front of the prison guards to convey secret messages and when she uses a quotation from Shakespeare "Sermons in stones" Sonny is elated to recognize the allusion and he finds in her a kindred spirit. Later, she writes to him, using a phrase "happy for battle" which Sonny finds both intriguing as well as mesmerizing, "so simple, so loaded, audacious, such a shocking, wild glorious juxtaposition of menace and elation, flowers and blood." (38)

She attends his trial regularly and when he is released, his relationship with her brings a new kind of joy—"the light of joy that illuminates long talk of ideas, not the 60-watt bulbs that shine on family matters." He finds in her both friend and lover, "everything that had remained hungry, stunted, half-realized, streamed towards her through opened gates." She fulfils his need for "erotic fun" and shows him that an ecstatic love affair is not at odds with the concentration of political activity. She is an exciting partner intellectually, challenging his thoughts, contributing to his ideas. In a way, it is a relationship superior to the state of marriage because it escaped the boring, humdrum pleasures of a "deadened life."

Paradoxically, a perverse desire to do the ordinary things that married people do, takes Sonny and Hannah to the cinema in a white suburb, where they come face to face with Will who has bunked studies to see a show. The encounter shakes both father and son to the core, though Sonny tries to remain composed outwardly. This is the beginning of Will's changing relationship with his father, his bitterness, anger and disgust, and his protectiveness towards his mother. Though both try to carry on normally, there is the burden of guilt and deceit between father and son. Moreover, Sonny still has to carry on his life with Aila, and the occasional sexual intimacy with her leaves him feeling drained and ashamed.

Sonny's need of Hannah is "terrible—in a magnificent way," but the intensity of their "perfect isolation" is by its very nature, doomed to end. Their trip to see the sunflower fields symbolizes this. They see only "a vast company of the dead" and when he picks a sunflower for her as a souvenir, it is a dead flower. Sonny's secret visits to Hannah entail embarrassing lying to be done to his comrades, so that when he leaves home, instead of euphoria, there is inside him, a surly unease. When he returns, he finds that his daughter, his favourite child, has cut her wrists in a suicide attempt.

Sonny's remorse leads him to experience fear and panic, and it is Hannah who, with her sympathetic and patient attitude, helps him to exorcize his guilt. "And tranquilly, because it was all one, in them, they turned from caresses to worried discussion about the action of police agent provocateurs among church groups in rent boycotts." (57) So now, "Sonny had no choice. Needing Hannah."

When Sonny sees Hannah in company where his wife Aila is also present, he has a heady sense of power, of possessing both at once. "Later, alone, desolated, shamed, he understood. He sought, even contrived, ways of appearing with his wife in houses where his other woman would be a guest. The sexual excitement of bringing the two women together entered him as a tincture, curling cloudy in a glass of water." (64)

Sonny now is part of the group making policy decisions and he is also one of their prime speakers, so it is he who is chosen to speak the oration at the cleansing of the graves ceremony for nine youngsters who have been shot by the police. As Hannah watches him speak, she is aware of his innate goodness and sincerity, his gift of spontaneity and his frankness. But the meeting is broken up when the police throw tear gas and fire shots.

As Hannah runs with the others, Sonny catches up with her, running "as if he were chained to her." (80) His fear for Hannah's safety makes him uncaring of anything else, so that, instead of stopping to help, he turns away from the bloodied body of a young boy who has been shot. But he makes "a terrible discovery," that because of personal selfishness, he has compromised his ideal of self-respect. "His face was distorted by anguish and incoherence" as he runs away with the crowd. Much later he relives this scene in his mind, the way in which his body had acted in obedience to instilled principles and forced its way through the crowd to the fallen young man, but just then a bullet had missed Hannah's head by inches and he had disobeyed his instinct and run. Though he tries to rationalize his failure by avowing that all action springs from self-preservation, he knows that in this case it has been only selfishness; in saving Hannah, he has really saved himself.

It is a shameful, secret realization which torments him, because he feels it may destroy their relationship which was "formed in a special and different morality." (87) But once again, Hannah provides a healing touch when she turns the matter into a generalized issue and gives him "safe passage to the open waters of generality."

When Sonny returns home he comes to learn that Baby has left home, to join the military wing of the movement. All his feelings are in turmoil as he sees Aila, quiet, dignified and harmless, yet with great sorrow in her face. For one moment, he has a terrible temptation to reveal everything before her. But he knows that there is nothing that he can share with her now, "needing Hannah." In his bitterness he remembers that Aila had done nothing to assuage his anguish at Baby's attempt to end her life. He had had to find comfort and understanding elsewhere. Now, he can do nothing for Aila.

"With Hannah he felt what he ought to feel," not guilty or ashamed, but proud and excited that his daughter should have done such an unexpected thing. His emotion translates itself into desire, because "needing Hannah—sexual happiness and political commitment were one." (86) Sonny is complacently aware that the sacrifice of a daughter is for him a part of his political commitment, but that for Aila, all was loss. "He had left her behind there." (95)

Both Sonny and Aila make a joint effort to keep up appearances, and so the familiar ritual of afternoon teas for the relatives continues. Sonny has political involvement to engage his whole being—"his judgement never lost touch with principle, while his unhesitating return to the struggle after detainment and imprisonment ensures that he was capable of bold pragmatism. With these credentials added to his intelligence and gifts as a speaker, he had emerged from among others to the company of decision-makers. There, the combination of his personality was reflected in his position: considered as one of the radicals, he was yet reassuring to the cautious; he could be used to press decisions in a form acceptable to them." (96) With Hannah, he argues and unravels his ideas, comrades united in a line of thought which sometimes unaccountably diverged.

But there is one occasion when, sitting with Hannah in the garden, he experiences an epiphanic moment, "the blurred rush of the chronology of living was halted for a while" and Sonny suddenly and ominously, becomes aware of the incongruity of his situation: "A rich white man's domain of quiet and beauty screened by green from screams of fear and chants of rage, from the filth of scrap-heap settlements and the smashed symmetry of shot bodies; he had no part in it. He did not know what he was doing there." (99)

In his absorption with his life with Hannah, Sonny has distanced himself from Aila to the extent that he does not know when and how she has acquired a passport and a visa and is planning to visit Baby. The information comes as a jolt to Sonny. His male ego only sees her as exercising her option of distancing herself from the struggle, but his subconscious mind is guilty with the knowledge of what he has done, that takes away his right to be in her place.

Hannah goes away because her grandfather has passed away, and now that Sonny is alone, he is restless, waiting impatiently for the phone calls. During the course of one such call, Hannah tells him that she has been declared a prohibited immigrant. Sonny mulls over several options for helping her, but all turn out to be futile. Another shock comes in the shape of a young man, sent by Hannah to stay in her house for a while. He introduces himself with the phrase that had become a kind of secret bond between Hannah and Sonny: "sermons in stones and good in everything" and Sonny senses that he is part of the underground. But he cannot get over the feeling that his private space has been invaded and that the very personal phrase should not have been used as a password in the mouth of a third person.

When Aila returns, she is full of the news of Baby's marriage and her pregnancy. Sonny feels hurt at her self-assurance, "for once she's taken responsibility for something all by herself" and when she gives instructions that the marriage was to be kept a secret, Sonny's male ego takes a blow. "Since when did Aila decide what was politically expedient? Since when did she think she understood such things? Did she really believe the Security Police weren't aware by now where Baby was and what she was doing?" (118) He tries to assert his superior knowledge in such matters: "Family life—babies—it doesn't go too well with activism like theirs. Doesn't really do, anywhere, but particularly in exile." But he is totally unaware of the reality of Aila's situation. He misinterprets it as merely a woman's joy at the idea of birth. And now that Aila has cut her long hair, he feels she is like any other woman now, and experiences a sense of exultation: "He's rid of Aila. Free." (119)

Sonny is increasingly involved in the ambiguities and intrigues that are growing in the movement and longs desperately for Hannah. However, he is unable to stop himself from expressing his displeasure at her giving the young man their secret password. Hannah is baffled at this show of mistrust; for her it was part of her involvement with the movement: "you don't live for each other, the loving is contained within the cause, and there would be no love if you were to refuse, because of personal risk, something expected of you by the struggle." (121) "You are the only friend I've ever had," she tells him.

Once again, Sonny reveals his impercipience and double standards when he speaks to Hannah about Baby: "Marriage implies certain social structures, and we're busy breaking up the existing ones, we have to, it's the task of our time, our children's time. I don't know why she wants it."

Sonny is involved in the disaffection brewing within the leadership and it is Hannah with whom he shares everything, "she was the one friend he ever had." But he is stunned when he comes to know that the needle of suspicion is pointed towards him, because he had once been approached by the group of disaffected comrades. He is filled with dismay that those whom he trusted so implicitly should have levelled these kinds of allegations about him. Hannah soothes him: "no one who matters can doubt your integrity for a moment," but Sonny knows that he had been labelled "unreliable" because of his serious involvement with Hannah. They knew Hannah: "One of themselves, in a way. But only in a way; not directly in the movement, certainly not acceptable as party to deliberations, decisions and tactics, and therefore not—most important—subject to discipline. . . . Sonny, who had been the most disciplined of men, knew that about her, however close he allowed her to come. And to come close to him was to come close to the movement. . . . He began to discern a shadow cast from Hannah. His needing Hannah." (132)

Once again, Sonny comes to realize that "nothing is simple in a life and a country where conflict breaks up all consistency of character." (135) He sees himself progressively marginalized, being given some high-sounding but minor responsibility in place of the ones he had fulfilled unsparingly. Though he does not complain, bowing to the decision of the tribunal, he knows that criticism is being levelled at him. Hannah tries to comfort him, but it does not satisfy him. He is irritated and ashamed of "this cosseting, he was her lover, not some victim to be succoured. . . . What he wanted, from her, was what no one could give him back; his trust in himself." (140)

Meanwhile Hannah has been recommended for the post of United Nations High Commission for Refugees Regional Representative for Africa. She is gratified at the esteem accorded to her, but worried at the implications for her relationship with Sonny. When, after much hesitation, she does give him the news, it is a facing of what she did not want to face. There is an imperceptible change between them—"everything became insidious between them, guilt and fear and regret taught her guile to save her skin form the corrosion of his pain." (145)

They decide to spend a week-end together, a weekend of reconciliation among the orange blossom. Sonny tells the necessary lies, to Aila, who still trusts him, and to his comrades, who seldom had any urgent need of him now. Once again, Sonny and Hannah discuss politics, but there is a new clarity in Hannah's perception: "A good man; her paradox was that what she revered in him was a trusting idealism she herself—whom she saw as a lesser being—questioned." (150)

But change is inevitable in any relationship—the law of life between a man and woman which makes a love affair inevitable, also obeys the other law of life, moving on. Both Sonny and Hannah know he would never leave Aila and his children; he would no longer be Sonny if he did. They both know that Hannah "lied by omission when she concealed from him under laconic practical references to her future post the excitement working in her at the idea of the vast continent of Africa." (150) So that it is a vain hope on Sonny's part when he feels that he would give her such love "that she could never forego it, never leave, needing Sonny."

When Sonny returns home after this weekend, he learns of Aila's arrest and that the police have found explosives hidden in their storeroom. Sonny is in a state of mental turmoil, but displays a great deal of courage. Even Will has to admit reluctantly "No man—no husband—could do more, even if he were to have loved my mother."

It is Hannah, however, who manages to find out where Aila was being held and to smuggle notes in and out. Sonny knows that whatever has happened has been because of this "woman in his arms," who has been the source of "ecstasy and hubris" and who had made him confident of being equal to all the demands of his temperament—dedication to liberation, maintenance of family, private passion, but who is now leaving him. The Shakespearean allusion comes to his mind: "O thou weed: who art so lovely faire, and smell'st so sweet that the sense aches at thee, Would thou had'st never been born"

But Sonny's obtuseness about Aila continues even when he is in the court waiting to see her produced before the judge. To him, she is still "poor Aila." He has been too preoccupied to notice so many things about Aila, her visits to 'friends from work' made him pleased to be relieved of responsibility for neglect, her visits to see her grandson were interpreted as sentimentalizing, Sonny just cannot accept that Aila too could have the intelligence and the guts to be a comrade-in-arms.

When Aila is granted bail, it is Sonny who takes her to the police station twice a day. But he still feels distress and denial at the preposterous idea of Aila a revolutionary responsible for her acts. But Sonny cannot wish away the facts. He sees the attention of the leadership is focused on her now. When Sonny expresses resentment at the fact that she had not discussed the matter with him before making her decisions, Aila is forthright: "I don't know whether I wanted to."

Sonny sees his whole life coming apart: "His attraction to Hannah belonged to the distorted place and time in which they—all of them—he, Aila, Hannah, lived. With Hannah there was the sexuality of commitment; for commitment implies danger, and the blind primal instinct is to ensure the species survives in circumstances of danger, even when the individual animal dies or the plant has had its season. In this freak displacement, the biological drive of his life, which belonged with his wife and the children he'd begotten, was diverted to his lover. He and Hannah begot no child; the revolutionary movement was to be their survivor. The excitement of their mating was for that. But Aila was the revolutionary, now " (169)

In this confused state of mind, Sonny's resentment turns against Hannah: "because of Hannah, Aila was gone. Finished off, that self that was Aila. Hannah destroyed it. Aila was gone too." Perversely, he yearns to escape "the cloying familiarity of marriage, to flee from it to the clandestine love wild and free from habit—and he longed unappeasably; nothing, nothing was there to stanch the longing for everything he had fled." (170)

Sonny knows he is having difficulty in accepting Aila as a comrade. He knows he has to make a conscious attempt to rid him of his outworn perception about Aila. He also knows that she had to be reinstated as his wife. But he has not understood the distance that Aila has travelled away from him. When she entreats bail and leaves the country, he has no prior knowledge of her plans. "So she did not need him, even for that." (183)

Sonny now has to come to terms with the fact that he is no longer of much importance in the movement, and the reason he knows was his preoccupation with a white woman. Though Sonny feels he has never neglected the cause for her, the leaders are united in their view that "There is no place for a second obsession in the life of a revolutionary." (184)

However, with both Aila and Hannah gone, circumstances force him into a life where he is "stripped of every obligation, every preoccupation, left for the cause alone." The political atmosphere is changing fast, more people are crossing the frontiers for openly political purposes, white extremism is rearing its ugly head, making blacks the target of vandalism. Sonny gets a chance to visit Lusaka as part of a delegation, but when he returns he learns that his house has been burned down. He remains undefeated, however: "We can't be burned out, he said, we're that bird, you know, it's called the phoenix, that always rises from the ashes." (192) As the novel ends, Sonny is back in the struggle and has been detained again.

In the character of Sonny, Gordimer presents, with great compassion, the trauma of failed idealism, a failure all the more tragic because it is brought about not only through personal weakness but through the circumstances of its times. Though Sonny feels that in his relationship with Hannah, he is able to merge the personal with the political so seamlessly that the differences of race and colour do not matter; it is a doomed relationship. Sonny's high-minded political commitment colours his involvement with Hannah, allowing him to see it as superior to the state of marriage because here, lover and cause were one. It also marks the emergence of hubris, for Sonny feels that his political commitment sets him apart from and even superior to "poor Aila," with her concern for family matters and ignorance of the world of political struggle. He violates the code of self-respect that he had instilled in his family by resorting to lies and evasions. He betrays the bond between a father and a son by forcing a confused Will into reluctant complicity with his extra-marital affair. He causes the break-up of a family and both Aila and Baby leave as if to compensate for the hurt he has caused to all by his abandonment of his duties as husband and father. And even though he is not fully aware of it, he dilutes his commitment to the cause. He is destroyed politically, for his relationship with a white woman is looked upon with suspicion and he is labelled as not entirely trustworthy. Yet the blame falls as much to the inequities of the society he inhabits as to him on the personal level, for he is the caged bird struggling to be free of a burdensome system.

Will

The narrator of the greater part of the story and as we come to know in the last chapter, the writer of this, his first book, Will's point of view, flawed and biased though it is, dominates. As the "son" he is both observer and participant in the action. In fact, the chain of events that set in motion the story, begins with Will's encounter with his father coming out of the cinema with a blonde white woman. Will has bunked studies during preparatory leave to see a film in a cinema in a far-off suburb, and the sudden meeting leaves him feeling shaken.

Will has been named after his father's favourite writer William Shakespeare and he has imbibed the ideals of 'self-respect' that governed the lives of his parents. Hence, he feels all the more keenly the betrayal of this ideal by his father. The women who inhabit his adolescent dreams are blonde, a fact made inevitable by the laws of segregation which decide their lives, but that fantasy has now been translated into the reality in which he sees his father caught in "the most vulgar, commonplace, shopworn of sticky traps."

Thus, Will's impressions of Hannah border on cruel mockery of "that broad pink expanse of face they have" her "bare pink bottle calves and clumsy sandals," so different from his mother with her groomed hair and elegant legs neatly crossed. But Will is still a child, and in the safety of his room, he "allows" himself to weep.

Will remembers a happy childhood, where the Sunday gatherings that he saw in neighbour's houses, replete with drinking and loud music, were not customary. Instead his family did things together, so that his life had security and warmth, "a charmed circle." His father teaches him how to repair gadgets and to play chess, takes him to the SPCA to choose a dog and opens up a world of storybooks for him. He teaches Will to read when he is less than 5 years old and Will loves to be read to by him. He finds strange and interesting things for Will—the skeleton of a fledgling caught by the fire, the cast of a songololo which can be used as a prism.

But all this magic is destroyed in one stroke that afternoon when Will, trying to "get lost in foreign territory," where no one would see him, where no one would know him, comes across what he had never expected to see: "he had shown me something I should never have been shown." (19) When Will gets back home, it is as if nothing had happened, his father behaves as normally as usual and Will is drawn into this complicity. In his confused state of mind he wonders: "And yet because he was my father how could I resist, how could I dare refuse him?" (20) But he relives the incident over and over again in his mind, and it brings further turmoil: "I did not know how to live now that I'd met him, now that I had seen, not the movie I bunked swotting for, but what our own life is." (24)

Will is burdened with his terrible knowledge and wants to tell his sister so that she will know what it is like to know and thus share his pain, instead of running round with her boyfriends and secretly smoking pot. The fact that his mother always has a special regard for his father's political commitment, makes Will ask bitterly: "What I'd like to know is does prison give my father the freedom to do what he's doing. Is it all right so long as she doesn't know." With his own growing sexual awareness he wonders how things are between his parents as husband and wife, especially after his father has come back from "the other one," who is "pink and thick and soft," like the blondes in his own sexual fantasies. It is something he has never given thought to before, and he does not want to think of it even now.

Will now sees himself in the role of a buffoon, aping his father's lies, "Poor Tom to his Lear." He wonders how his father managed, when they were alone in their bedroom. Will's worries are for his mother. Though she seems to him as she always had been, he is afraid for her. He wants her to still think of his father in her "gentle, trusting way." (40) It leads him to hide the dried sunflower head lying in the car, which he senses belongs to the other woman as a way of protecting his mother from hurt. This compounds his confusion and he does not know what to do, whether to keep out of her way, or to be with her to cover up that his father wasn't.

Initially Will is sure that his mother has no knowledge of the matter. Even at the time when they had had a party at home in honour of the men who had been released from prison, it is she who suggests that Hannah Plowman's name be included in the list of invitees. Will has a nagging thought that she had done this out of some sort of guile, to test his father's reaction, but immediately dismisses it as unworthy of his mother. It hurts to have such thoughts: "But when you are lying, in your presence at the table, in every expression on your face, in everything you customarily do, . . . you can't imagine anything that isn't devious, anymore. The whole world is lying, fornicating and lying." (41) His dislike of Hannah conditions his attitude to her looks "pink scrubbed face, blonde hair springing back into shape like the coat of a wet dog," and contrasting her with his own mother with a pretty comb in her "tight and shiny crown of hair, she was neat and beautiful, with the special care she took to dress for parties."

When Baby cuts her wrists during one of his father's absences, Will finally understands that Baby, too, knew, it was just that she managed her knowledge differently, her brash vulgar style and emotional outbursts were all her way of coping, and attempting suicide when she could not cope. He also understands that his mother knew, too and that she knew that Will knew, too. His resentment against his father boils over: "What a family he made of us."

In his childish fury, Will wants to knock over the glass of water in his father's hand when he returns. He contrasts his father's negligence with his own devotion: "I was with her, had been with her ever since it happened, he had to face me." (52) All his submerged resentment against his father surfaces; he knows Baby is his father's favourite child, "even though he quoted Shakespeare to me and wanted me to bring him glory by growing up to be a writer just to please him." (53) Will has a fit of cruelty in which he wants to take out the dried sunflower and fling it at his father, because he can't stand the way he has been let off his misery so easily.

When Baby recovers she tries to give her version of what happened, but Will knows it is clearly a performance, Baby was covering up for her father, and Will feels she is as devious and lying as he is.

Their lives settle down to an "uncanny sort of normality, an acceptance of the rearrangement of our lives tc his convenience." Will is even sent to Hannah's house with a package of books, so that he sees the place his father goes to, so different from their own house, his father giving, Will notes sarcastically, "a perfect performance" in front of his mother as he sends Will off on his new motorcycle

Will experiences a kind of loathing when he thinks of Hannah: "She reminds me of pig." (64) And inevitably, come the thoughts of sex. Though Will hates himself for it: "I'm sick with myself. What's he made me think about." His mind keeps going round and round about what he has seen, the underwear on the radiator, and he curses himself for having ever allowed her to enter their house: "Stupid kid that I was. The man of the house. They bring you up to be polite and then put you in situations they didn't tell you could ever happen."

Will's confused mind tries to find reasons for being sent to Hannah's place. Sometimes he feels that his father has done it deliberately so that he could have a partner in guilt. "Now he wants me to see her, see what he enjoys and be guilty with him of what he feels because I understand it in myself." At other times, he feels it is because his father wants to show off his virility, his sexual prowess in possessing two women at the same time, as he crudely puts it, "The old bull still owns the cows." And he is overwhelmed by the burden of his isolation and pain: "I don't think my father knows any of these things about himself, Only I know, only I."

Will's paranoia makes him suspicious of every move made by his parents. With his knowledge comes a sense of power: "They have nothing private from me, now." (83) He feels doubly protective towards his mother: "my attention is a bit like an ordinary old pocket torch that I hold, walking backwards before her as she manages to keep to her way in its light." He also realizes that he has become a bundle of contradictions—behaving in a way that would have been unthinkable earlier, snooping into other people's private belongings, so that he knows exactly what is in the carry-all that Aila hands over to Sonny.

Will's tensions lead him to experience an inferiority complex, where, though he has gained three distinctions and a university pass in his examinations, he still feels hurt to believe that his parents, even his mother, are prouder of Baby (who has joined the revolutionary movement and left home), than of him. Thus, he looks for the psychological satisfaction of seeing his mother's face giving confirmation that without him, she felt deserted.

The ritual of Saturday afternoon teas continue, but Will now learns new things about his parents—that it is his mother who lied when she told the relatives that Baby was overseas, and that, when he sees his father giving respect and support to relatives who still live in the ghetto, he still feels a rush of love for him, something he does not understand. Moreover, he learns that Hannah, whom he so dislikes, is known to the comrades of the movement as a "good girl," that is, someone who could be relied upon to know the priorities; so that now he is in a bind: "If his woman were not a good girl it would be all right for me to loathe her." (94)

Will also comes to know by accident, that his mother has had passport photographs taken and when Aila leaves for Lusaka, ostensibly to see Baby, he sees his father spend most of his time at home. He is uncertain whether this is something his mother had instructed Sonny to do, or whether he really wanted to be with him. One evening, as he returns home late, Will hears voices of several men, and later his father warns him not to speak of this to anyone. Will senses that there is trouble brewing in the organization.

When his mother returns, she has cut her hair and Will almost does not recognize this woman with the dull permed hair. He senses a change in her that is irrevocable: "Cut loose. She was gone for good: my mother." (116)

The news that Baby is going to have a child once again stirs up Will's simmering disgust and anger: "Fucking his pudding faced blonde (pink blancmange like my mother used to make for us out of a packet when we were kids) while he ought to be dandling his grandchild on his knee. It's disgusting to think like this about him, I know, but he's the one who's brought it about." He feels that self-esteem, if not self-respect, and some shred of dignity, should have stopped his father from continuing with his relationship.

Will sees his mother going to visit Baby, making baby clothes to take with her, but his obtuseness is evident when he remarks that the doctor for whom his mother works does not seem to object to her taking frequent absences. He thinks she must be taking unpaid leave, yet wonders that she is able to save money for air fares. Will notices many things that have changed in his mother—the fact that she does not dress with the same care as before, the fact that she seems to have made more friends, friends of her own and not his father's, with whom she was always on the fringe. With a heavy heart, Will realizes: "She was not there. Not for him, not for me." (124)

Will now has a girl friend, but he still cannot bring himself to move in with her, because he feels responsible for his mother: "I can't leave my mother alone, and because my mother counts on me to be there with him when she's away, I can't leave him." He notices that his father now counts for less among his peers than before, that the leaders of the movement don't come round for talks so often. But so far as his mother is concerned, Will remains impercipient—he continues to think that his mother is compensating for the void in her life and what she must feel about her husband, through her visits to Baby and her grand-child.

Will wonders where his mother has picked up "jargon" like "Bush fighters won't win the economic war. . . . You're valuable, Will." (130) Because he sees himself as both accomplice and protector, he believes she is really saying indirectly: "don't leave. Don't leave me. Don't leave us." Though he notices that his mother seems to have become more independent of his father, Will once again misinterprets his mother's changed behaviour: "she just wanted to show me she cannot live with him, without me." (131)

Will is at first irritated and then embarrassed when phone calls start coming, asking for his mother. Once again, his biased mind clouds his perception. He jumps to the conclusion that his mother, too, could be having an affair and magnanimously exonerates her of guilt: "My poor mother with her ugly shorn head and her brave show of having a life of her own, knitting baby clothes and trying to make new friends among her employer's patients. I'm old enough now, almost to wish it were true. I understand the reassurance to be found in a stranger to whom one is something, someone, outside the triangle—father, mother, son; Sonny, Aila, Will—of this house." (138)

But Will's bland assessment of his mother is turned upside down the night the police raid their house to arrest her. Will watches in horror as she calmly answers to her name when they interrogate her, and readies the bag used by his father when he went to prison. His first reaction is to blame his father: "The bastard! That bastard, what has he done now! What has he done to get you inside! I'll kill him." (144) After his mother has been taken away, Will, in a frenzy, rushes to Hannah's house to find his father and kill him: "he's the one, who, once again, wasn't there." He finds the house empty and is almost shot as an intruder.

But rage dies down in the face of the terrible reality. Will accompanies his father to the lawyer and then to police headquarters to find out where Aila is being held. To some extent, Will does this out of a sense of commitment to his mother: "I knew what she would ask me to do." (154) It is also his commitment to his father: "it's nobody's business—except his and mine." His conflicting feelings surface; on the one hand he blames his father "if anything happens to her it's his doing." On the other, he sees that "No man—no husband—could do more, even if he were to have loved my mother."

When Will sees the signed statement in which Aila admits to have knowledge of the hidden cache of "property" but does not reveal the names of those who had entrusted them to her, he realizes that she has been briefed on how to deal with interrogators. He is stunned at how she could have "come to kinds of knowledge that were not for her." At the same time, he is "elated" and a kind of release soars up within him. "She was in prison and she was free, free of him, free of me." (156) But harsh reality intrudes. He knows this freedom is illusory. She was shut inside prison.

Will goes with his father to meet Aila, and he senses his father's discomfiture at the sudden realization that Aila was not "innocent" a word that in his usage meant "denying responsibility towards your own people." Will feels that there are many things that he could have told his father, things he didn't have time to notice and most importantly that "he was mistaken in his demeaning decision (typical! Of course only his blonde has the intelligence and guts to be a comrade-in-arms) that she was manipulated, beguiled into use by Baby and that husband." (163) As Will sees a special "machinery" move in to take care of Aila's bail plea and he realizes that it is not only his father, but his mother, too, who had been leading a secret life and that he, in a way, has been a cover for both of them.

When Aila returns home, everything centres on her, the attention of the leadership is focused on her. During the course of the meetings held at their house, Will comes to hear that Hannah has gone away. He immediately draws the mocking conclusion that his father is now the good husband, the good comrade only because "that woman" has gone, that he is home now because there was no more big bed on the floor for him. Wil! makes a trip to Hannah's house just to make sure, but it does not give him the sensation that he seeks: "I didn't find exorcism then and there." (167)

Will attends the court session in which the evidence against Aila is produced. He is horrified to see, apart from the hand grenades and limpet mines that had been found in their outhouse, other objects, an RPG-7 rocket launcher and two rockets. Will suddenly feels "immensely important." It is his evidence that would expose their lies and trickery and set his mother free. "He is elated to have an identity of his own: "I was nobody's conspirator. I had found my own point of reference through my own experience." (174)

At the same time, Will is filled with a new and disturbing knowledge—that Aila had always known what was in that outhouse and had not wanted her son to know. His confidence in himself and the bond of intimacy he feels he had with his mother is shaken and the final blow comes when Aila refuses to have Will give evidence. Will's anger finds a mark when he sees his father squeeze Aila's shoulder and let his hand lie a moment. "Is he telling little wifey it's all right, she has her strong clever leader-of-the-people husband, turned up at last to talk her out of her foolish notions?" Will sees his father trying to convince Aila to change her mind and put to rest any doubts that she has about Will's safety: "Would I lie to you?," he says. Will feels like bursting into laughter, to say "yes, yes, and yes again," but neither he nor his mother react. When Aila speaks, "It's enough. It's enough," it is as though she speaks to both father and son. Will senses her meaning: "My father the famous Sonny, Baby the revolutionary exile. Aila the accomplice of Umkhonto weSizwe: they are our family's sacrifice for the people," but again, his biased mind seething with the pain of what he perceives to be a betrayal, makes him give another twist to her words: "there's no need of me, who needs someone like me? They are the heroes."

What Will does not understand is that his mother has enough to bear without having her boy involved in any way. When he takes his mother to task about this, her reply is clear: "I don't want you mixed up in this. I don't want your life decided by mine." (178) But Will finds this attitude unbearable. He bursts out in a long tirade:

> Why do I have to say this again? Why must I be the one excepted, the one left behind, left out, why is it assumed—by you, by him, by Baby, everyone—I haven't any part in the struggle? Why is it just accepted I'm the one who lives the sham normal life you've all rejected, I'm to be happy on the edge of the white man's world of big business, money, going to be smugly settled in a year or two in some big firm or multinational if there're any left here, given loans to build a house just as good as theirs where they say I can. Driving a company car, marrying some girl presentable enough by their standards for their annual dinner, producing kids I can afford to send to some private school that takes kids like ours—why?. Why is it decided that that's for me? Who de-

> cided it? What's wrong with me? Why me? Is there some birthmark or something that says this is what I must be?
>
> . . . It's like a curse, I'm supposed to take it as my fate. And now you, you, when I can act like the rest of you, when I can face them in court and tell them they're liars, liars, those thugs who've been let into our house—and I let them in, I'm the one who's let every kind of destruction into our house, I'm always there, handy, Will is going to do it, well named, he'll do it—now you say, It's enough. Enough! There's nothing for me in the struggle to change our lives. I'm needed at home. I am home. It's enough! I've had enough of it.
>
> . . . What's so special about me? So I'm your stake in something, I'm to be something you and he don't really want to give up? Not even for the revolution? The token place in the boardroom you don't really, somewhere in you—you don't want to destroy? Am I your hostage, your middle-class nostalgia for nice things?

Will unburdens himself of all his pent-up grievances and feels that his mother has no way of stopping him from telling the truth. But as they walk down the street towards their home, they see a dead cat hanging on their gate with a piece of cardboard lettered BLACK COMMUNIST BITCH GET OUT OF HERE. Will's resentment vanishes and with their arms round each other, in a demonstration of closeness, he and his mother walk up the path and into the house.

On Tuesday, the fourteenth of June, Will comes home to find his mother gone again, and this time, neither he nor his father have any idea of her whereabouts. It is only when a young girl, garishly made-up and dressed like a smart little garment factory worker on her way to work, comes and delivers a note from one of the comrades in the leadership, that they know about her. Seeing this girl, Will feels a sense of pride at the unguessed-at commitment of ordinary people to the struggle, hidden under that cheap appearance. He feels he should be the one to tell white folks that they don't know what they are seeing when they look at ordinary black men and women.

Will stays behind at home to be there when the police come looking for Aila. He feels a sense of release and elation in the thought that Aila is free of all the constraints that burden their lives—the unfair laws and police oppression.

As time passes, Will is busy with his studies in business administration. Now, there is a renewed and unspoken bond with his father. When Sonny returns from a trip to Lusaka, Will receives him at the airport with the news that their house has been burned down. Earlier, he had come home to find a big crowd in front of the house staring at placards with racist slogans and with a crude drawing of Sonny slashed across with thick red strokes. As Will fights his way through the mass of people, they shout at him Wat maak jy hier? What are you doing here? The police disperse the mob, but that night, someone petrol-bombs the house.

Will goes with his father to look at the blackened bricks and timber, the shattered ice-floes of glass. He sees his father poking at the rubble, breathing fast and loud in anger and close to tears. But while Sonny rhetoricizes about renewal, for Will what dominates is the smell of smoke: "that was the smell of her. The smell of destruction, of what has been consumed, that he first brought into that house." (192)

In the last chapter, Will muses about his relationship with his father which encompassed both love and hate. He talks of the way this story has been built up, personal experience, memory, imagination—all have gone into it. Sometimes he has used "the license of hindsight," sometimes he has realized that his own opinions and judgements, his own voice has intruded in what should have been other people's.

The chip on his shoulder that he has carried all through now surfaces once again as he looks forward to his own time in politics: "I was excluded from that, it didn't suit them for me to have any function within it, but I'm going to be the one to record, someday, what he and my mother, Aila and Baby and the others did, what it really was like to live a life determined by the struggle to be free."

Will writes down a poem that he has written for his father who has been detained again, the imagery of bird and stone walls defining the idea of freedom and death. He knows that it is his experience that has motivated his writing, so that in a way it was what his father did that has made him a writer. But given the circumstances of the times, it is a book that will never be published.

Through the character of Will, Gordimer traces a pattern of turbulent adolescence with its fierce loyalties, bitter disenchantments and searing sexual awakenings. Will's role as man-of-the-family after his father's arrest and his special care and concern for his mother intensifies as he is drawn, reluctantly and helplessly, into an involvement with his father's affair with Hannah. As horrified observer and sarcastic commentator, Will provides the entry point for the reader through the complexities of response that govern a situation where simple judgements can be misleading. For Will himself, the experience is cathartic, for as he matures he is able to overcome his adolescent resentments and see things from a broader viewpoint. He is led to understand the high price to be paid by those involved in the freedom struggle and his own role in it.

Aila

Aila, the girl Sonny marries, with her "coiled river of shining black hair" seems to be set apart for him in her beauty and elegance. Her nature is so reserved that the young men around her feel that her beauty is wasted and do not quite know what to make of her. Aila did not flirt; it was not possible to have sexual thoughts about her. They mistook her gentleness for disdain, instead of recognizing it for what it was—strength of will, softly gloved. For Aila, a husband meant a lifelong friend and lover, and while she gave Sonny everything of herself, she kept to herself some fibre of her personality as a separate identity. Sonny did not know what exactly this was, but it added respect to his love for her.

There is a great bond of passion, sensitivity, even telepathy between Aila and her husband. She wanted to become what he wanted and so she took a secretarial course and studied psychology by correspondence in preparation for a useful working life. Aila, too, makes self-respect her code of conduct, so that when Sonny is in prison and she is visited by Hannah, representative of a human rights organization, whose job is to help the families of the detainees, it is as if her well-groomed hair and elegant neatly crossed send out a message of self-sufficiency.

The 'charmed circle' Sonny and Aila draw round their children becomes a part of the mutual bond that unites the two: "For what she wanted was, in essence, always what he wanted." (13) Will feels he can never quite understand, for this was not something submissive. Aila's breeding and elegance extends to the lunches and teas she hosts for their relatives, spending the whole of Saturdays to prepare the traditional dishes that had come down to her, her oriental beauty half hidden by her neat blouses and skirts.

Aila knows all about Sonny's growing involvement in political matters, and like any mother her fears are for her children. As Sonny plans to move into a white neighbourhood as part of the resistance program, he is aware that to do so would be an uprooting of the "organic order and aesthetic discipline of Aila's life." (26) Yet, Aila supports him in every decision, and presents this move to the children as something exciting and desirable. Aila understands everything and Sonny can keep nothing from her. "Because she said little herself, she did not depend on words for the supply of information from others."

But things change when Sonny comes out of prison, for now there is something that Aila has not gone through with him. Even during his imprisonment, Aila visits him, dressed carefully and elegantly, as if to reassure him that everything was all right at home. But for Sonny, the talk of family matters does not seem to satisfy him. The silences which he found so comfortable at home, now become real silences without communication.

Aila visits him only occasionally, because she is conscientious: "it was an article of faith between Sonny and her, part of her loyalty and support for him, in prison, that they would not let the State destroy the discipline of their daily lives." (35) So she brings him jackets and trousers fresh from the dry-cleaners, so that the prisoner could stand in court with his morale high. She attends the court sessions with the families of the accused and during the break, he holds her hands folded together in his, because their intimacy has always been too private for public display of kissing. But when Sonny is sentenced, Aila breaks through her reserve and kisses him full in the mouth in front of the warders. Sonny sees that in order not to shame him, she pretends not to see the tears rise in his eyes. She also smoothes her hair in a gesture of courageous defiance.

However, Sonny betrays her trust and support when he starts comparing her with Hannah. Her letters full of family matters arouse in him a sense of dissatisfaction: "Why did Aila never speak? Why did she never say what he wanted her to say?"

Aila's life seems to move on an even pace even as Sonny's passionate involvement with Hannah Plowman grows. To Will, her son, the fact that she has known of this relationship for quite a while becomes clear when Baby cuts her wrists during one of Sonny's now frequent absences from home. Young as he is, Will senses the change—she could no longer count on him, "couldn't call on Sonny." (42)

The deception is made easier for Sonny because Aila is not a demanding woman sexually and so their sexual encounters are not frequent. Nevertheless, on the rare occasions that he forces himself to make love to her, he is ashamed and angry with himself and, quite irrationally, with her.

The very fact that Aila carries on as if everything was the same, that she has not disturbed her habits, becomes an irritant for Sonny. He does not realize the depth of her concern for him and is surprised when she hands him a carry-all containing clothing and other essentials as he leaves home for his oration at the "cleansing of the graves" ceremony. Though Sonny feels nothing, Will is more perceptive. He knows that the things in that bag represent her fears, "that he might be taken away next time as he was the first, without the means to keep himself clean—the means of self-respect so important to him—and warm: the pull-over is her means of love, whether that's important to him or not." (83)

When Baby joins a military wing of the movement, it is to Aila that she first breaks the news. Aila takes it in her stride, but Sonny notices that there is "great sorrow in her face" and he could not be sure it was for him. His male ego dismisses her as "poor Aila." There are many things he doesn't notice, because of his obtuse idea that Aila was not a priority because she was not in the struggle. He feels he has left her behind, because his political commitment has provided him with a refuge while "for Aila, all was loss. There was no gain." (94) Sonny measures the distance that has crept into their relationship: "Aila could do nothing for him. He could do nothing for Aila."

So it comes as a shock to Sonny to learn that Aila the "stay-at-home wife and mother" had arranged for a passport and visa and was going to visit Baby. In his obtuseness, Sonny only feels envy at the ease with which she is able to distance herself from the struggle.

When Aila returns, Will sees with a shock that she has cut her hair and her "dull permed curls" remind him forcibly that she had cut herself loose from them: "She was gone for good: my mother." (116) For Sonny, too, it marks a chapter closed in their life: "She'll never sit at the dressing table before bed, brushing that long, straight shining hair again. He's rid of Aila. Free." (119)

Sonny still retains his patronizing stance, however: "for once she's taken responsibility for something all by herself." But even he notices a change in Aila, he finds her taking charge with a new confidence that he finds irritating: "Since when did Aila decide what was politically expedient? Since when did she think she understood such things?" (118)

Aila goes to visit Baby and her little grandchild often, carrying baby clothes. Will notices that the doctor for whom his mother worked did not seem to object to her taking frequent absences, but he interprets it as being unpaid leave: "but my mother is used to managing with little money, she doesn't skimp us, in the household, and yet apparently she is able to save enough for the airfares." He notices other changes, too, but does not attach any particular importance to them—the fact that his mother no longer dresses with the care she did earlier and that she has made friends of her own, so that she is often out. He feels his mother is lost to them: "She was not there. Not for him, not for me."

Aila is happy to meet Will's girlfriend, because she would like to see him settled in a conventional domestic life. But for Will, it is a role that rankles: "tame Will keeps the home fires burning while noble Sonny and Baby defend the freedom of the people." When he protests, Aila reasons with him: "We're going to need qualified people. Bush fighters won't win the economic war." (130) Will is startled to hear his mother talking in this way: "Where does my mother get that kind of jargon? . . . She and I don't communicate like that." But like Sonny, Will's ego blinds him to many things about his mother. He notices that she has become more independent of his father, that she goes out to meet friends on her own, but he misinterprets this as a brave front put on by her. And this misconception leads him to jump to the conclusion that his mother, too, must have a lover, when he picks up phone calls where a male voice asks for his mother. Because Will can never imagine any role for his mother other than what he has been so long used to seeing, his reaction is one of ironic sympathy: "My poor mother with her ugly shorn head and her brave show of having a life of her own, knitting baby clothes and trying to make new friends among her employer's patients. . . . I understand the reassurance to be found in a stranger to whom one is something, someone." (138)

When the police come to arrest Aila, it is, once again, Will who is at home with her. But when Sonny returns, Will's anger dies out, and he accompanies his father to the police stations in search of Aila, because he knows that that is what she would want him to do. For the first time, both father and son face the stunning fact that Aila was deeply involved in activities that had led to detention and imprisonment, that she had talked under interrogation in order to protect her husband and son, and that she had been briefed on how to deal with interrogators.

Their biased attitudes extend to their disbelief that Aila could ever be a prisoner of conscience: ("Aila in that role") or to ever imagine that the freedom songs and salutes could be for "poor Aila." But when she comes out to meet them, they all notice that "through the familiar beauty there was a vivid strangeness boldly drawn. As if some chosen experience had seen in her, as a painter will in his subject, what she was, what was there to be discovered. In Lusaka, in secret, in prison—who knows where—she had sat for her hidden face. They had to recognize her." (161)

Now both Sonny and Will realize that Aila does not need their comforting words, for "there were no fears for him to still or tears for him to wipe." (162) There is a bond between Aila and her lawyer that is "the ease of two who have established confidence in a matter of survival." And the changed Aila does not have the time or thought to ask how things were at home.

Aila is charged with four offences under the Internal Security Act. The charges include terrorism and furthering the aims of a banned organization. She is accused of being a member of something called the Transvaal Implementation Machinery, responsible for acts of terror in the region and connected to a high command named Amos Seboking. She is accused of having acted as a courier between Umkhonto weSizwe in neighbouring countries and a cell in the Johannesburg area, of having attended meetings where the missions for the placing of explosives were planned and to have concealed terrorist arms on the rented property where she is said to be residing illegally.

Now Sonny has to accept the fact that Hannah's phrase "happy for battle" applies just as much to Aila as to himself. But he does not understand the implications until he sees Hannah weeping at the thought of Aila betrayed and feels "a dire displacement." (165)

Everything starts centring round Aila, the attention of the leadership is now focused on her. As Aila busies herself preparing for her trial, Sonny comes to realize that what had earlier appeared to him as preposterous was now the reality. Aila was a revolutionary responsible for her acts, a revolutionary who with total inner certainty had chosen her path, who, according to her, had "understood" the necessity for what she had done. His male ego rankles at the indefinable "something that appears disappearing from his grasp," his subconscious irritation that Aila should have taken this step without discussing it with him. But Aila puts their changed relationship into focus when she answers: "I don't know whether I wanted to." The change is also painfully obvious to Sonny when he notices that Aila faked her pleasure during love-making, that she was thinking of something else.

When matters take a turn during Aila's trial with the revelation made by Will that the RPG-7 rocket launcher and two rockets displayed by the prosecution were not initially part of the objects discovered by the police during their search in their outhouse, Sonny is elated that the case would be dismissed. But, once again, Aila stuns everybody by her firm insistence that Will should not give evidence. "It's enough. It's enough," she says; Will realizes that this is her way of protecting him, "her child" but it only leaves him feeling embittered for being sidelined. Aila explains: "I don't want you mixed up in this. I don't want your life decided by mine." (178) But Will, angry and frustrated at what he feels are the double standards Aila is maintaining—talking of revolution on the one hand and making him hostage to her middle-class nostalgia for the nice things of life—is unreasonably cruel, until he sees the dead cat hanging at their gate with the placard "BLACK COMMUNIST BITCH GET OUT OF HERE." It restores the sense of protectiveness that he had always felt for his mother.

But neither Will nor his father is prepared for what they see as Aila's obstinacy or obduracy, rather. This aspcct of her nature is so different from what she had been earlier, that for Sonny it becomes inexplicable. But the shattering reality permeates when Aila entreats bail and leaves the country without the knowledge of either her husband or her son. He comes to know of the extent of Aila's involvement with the resistance struggle and her commitment to it. Aila had performed her missions commendably, but now her cover was blown. Her name would be honoured, from now on in the movement inside and outside the country—where she could still be active.

For Will, this is the second time that his mother had gone away and never come back. "Now Aila is gone, and she won't come back until everything here is changed, she will not be judged by the laws white men made for us." (183) Though occasional phone calls come from far away countries and Sonny gets to hear Aila's voice, he senses the excitement in that voice rise when she talks to Will.

Assessing Aila's character, Malashri Lal writes: "Aila, though denied an active voice in *My Son's Story*, emerges as the most memorable figure. . . . Within her seeming inactivity and domesticity, she makes her political affiliations at a much higher level than Sonny and takes greater risks." (Introduction, xvi)

Through the character of Aila, Gordimer lauds all those unassuming women who sacrificed their personal happiness for the cause or who were forced to take up unexpected roles due to the pressures of the political environment. Moving from out of Sonny's shadow, Aila takes up an active part in a society in the throes of turbulent change, without losing anything of her womanliness. To the very end, she remains the dignified wife and loving mother, ready to make the ultimate sacrifice rather than jeopardize the safety of her child. Her outer calm and detachment hide a deep inner strength, one that deceived even those closest to her. Her heroism is not as obvious as Sonny's, yet it is more daring. In her, the personal and the political do not conflict, and her commitment to both her worlds is nurturing rather than destructive.

Hannah

Hannah Plowman is the white woman whose love affair with Sonny provides the catalyst for Will's story. She is a representative of a human rights organization monitoring political trials and she comes into contact with Sonny during the course of his detention and court appearances and with his family when she visits them to enquire about their welfare.

Her maternal grandfather was an Anglican missionary in one of the British protectorates on the borders of the country who had stayed back after his retirement and even after the country's independence. Her mother had studied nursing in Rhodesia and come back to the mission pregnant and given birth to a girl child—Hannah. Later she found out that her father was a Bulawayo policeman who was already married. Hannah's education was financed by another grandfather who had made good, holding important positions. Her mother married a Jewish doctor who was also an art collector and Hannah spent part of her school holidays in her grandfather's mud-brick and thatch house at the mission and part in Cape Town with her stepfather.

In Cape Town Hannah comes into contact with young people from well-off white families who had committed themselves to social service, working with trade unions, legal aid bureaus, human rights projects in squatter camps. She comes to view the social situation in a more realistic manner, unlike her earlier childish view that all Southern Africa was home. Now she is aware of boundaries, treaties, barbed wire, heavily armed border posts. (60)

Her commitment to political struggle receives impetus from her grandfather's commitment to struggle against evil in men, for God. For her, the drive becomes a struggle against it for man—for humans. She marries a young lawyer, but they soon part. She works for trusts, foundations, organizations which pay very little, but for her this poverty is a choice, for if she had wanted to, she would have been set up in other paying careers by her relatives.

Hannah's work with people who have devoted their lives and sacrificed everything for the cause opens up to her a new world. Her experience of their "divine strength" heightens her emotional resources, and associating with prisoners of conscience creates a special climate in which this heightening infloresces. She was in love. Not in the conventional sense, but in the sense of "a temperature and atmospheric pressure of shared tension, response, the glancing contact of trust in place of caresses, and the important, proud responsibility of doing anything asked, even the humblest tasks, in place of passionate private avowals. A loving state of being." (61-62)

It is in this state that she develops the persistence, the ability to lie boldly and threaten, with complete lack of scruple, to initiate international action, so as to pressurize the prison authorities to allow her to see detainees. And thus she meets Sonny.

Long after their relationship has deepened into love, Sonny remembers her as he first saw her during her visit to prison, blonde, with a big face, soft pink, whose bone structure was not evident, rough-cut curly hair, sturdy legs with lightly freckled calves. Narrow blue eyes, the kind that do not have much depth or variety of expression, like the glass-bright eyes fixed so realistically in furry stuffed toys which yet hold attention by their surface colour. Layers of garments piled over each other in a careless kind of way, neither graceful nor well-dressed. Yet there is a radiance about her as she cleverly steers double-talk past the warders. Talking about food, she lets him know indirectly that some of the comrades were on hunger strike, or relating a weather report she is able to indicate where other comrades are being held.

Later Sonny gets a letter from Hannah in which the apparently innocuous message is layered with hidden meaning. And the letter ends with a line "I know you'll come out happy for battle." The three words touch him deeply, they contain her uncanny ability to represent his whole life. He finds that phrase "so simple, so loaded, audacious, such a shocking, wild, glorious juxtaposition of menace and elation, flowers and blood, people sitting in the sun and bodies dismembered by car bombs, the harmonized singing coming from somewhere in the cells, and the snarl of a police dog leaping at his face, once, in a crowd." (38)

Their next meeting is after a debriefing session in which Sonny is one of the speakers. They meet afterwards for coffee and Sonny looks at Hannah's face more openly than before. He sees her "Thick-fleshed, pearly-skinned modelling with slight scuffed redness here and there when her fingernail or some rough cloth had brushed it; the defining presence in the colour of the eyes." She gives him her scarf to shield him from the cold, and Sonny feels a sense of joy even from something so slight as this.

They are friends first and later lovers, but it is as if a mutual need has been fulfilled in their union. Hannah is open and honest about their relationship and one of the things that Sonny finds specially appealing about her is that she has no wish to oust Aila from his mind. Sonny feels a sense of gratitude for this—"No guilt, no concealment between them, with her, everything that had remained hungry, stunted, half-realized, streamed towards her through open gates." (46)

But Hannah feels "a strange threat of loss in the midst of joy" the first time she makes love to Sonny, because she is painfully aware of a change. The earlier "loving state of being" with which she had met Sonny's family has been "terrifyingly transformed" by passion.

Needing Hannah—the phrase becomes a constant refrain in Sonny's mind, as she opens up for him a magical world. Partly, the attraction stems from the fact that Hannah, too, is someone who is "in the battle, for whom the people in the battle are her only family, her life, the happiness she understands." (46) Hannah knows a lot of poetry and Sonny learns about the room which is "an everywhere," a phrase (from John Donne) which aptly translates his own feelings. She is his companion not only in the sexual sense, but intellectually, challenging his thoughts as he knows Aila could never have done. In fact, Sonny finds Hannah quite different from other women, she has no need for the paraphernalia of home-making; her bed is only a big mattress on the floor and her home decorations consist of a big modern painting on the wall and a reproduction of Van Gogh's painting of sunflowers in her kitchen.

Their mutual dedication to a political ideal and battle heightens their concentration and application in such matters and at the same time brings about the roused state of an ecstatic love affair. But the fact that their love affair is clandestine, that they cannot do the ordinary things that lovers do, makes them hanker for common shared pleasures and it is in the course of one such outing to see a film together, that Sonny and Hannah run into Will, who has bunked studies to visit the cinema. The encounter shakes all concerned. Hannah is afraid. "She saw how he had changed: how she had changed him without knowing." (50) But she is too perceptive to be complacent when Sonny assures her that Will had not mentioned anything at home, it's as if it never happened. All she says, however, is "That can't be."

The cleansing of the graves ceremony finds Hannah in the combi along with the other white supporters and she feels a sense of pride in Sonny, in his goodness, sincerity and frankness. But when the police fire into the crowd, she is carried along with the wave of people running to escape the tear-gas and bullets. She finds herself being pulled along by Sonny, but for a while they manage to get back to where a boy lay shot through the head. But the pressing mass of people push them away, a bullet misses Hannah's head by inches and Sonny disobeys the principles he has so far espoused by turning away and running with Hannah in tow.

When Sonny hears of Baby's decision to join the movement, his pride and excitement are echoed by Hannah. When she goes back to Lesotho on the death of her grandfather, Sonny waits every third day for her phone calls. He learns that Hannah has been declared a prohibited immigrant and he knows that it will be difficult for her to come back. He is startled, therefore, when he sees a young man at her house who introduces himself with the same password 'Sermons in stones' that had become a private love-code between Hannah and himself. He reproaches Hannah for the risks this could entail, but for Hannah, love was only a part of the cause, "there would be no love if you were to refuse, because of personal risk, something expected of you by the struggle." (121) Hannah's generous nature is able to understand the complexities of life and the difficulties of choice, and though Sonny does not tell her that he has now become a grandfather, nothing would have changed for her had he done so, she would only have felt her share in his life enriched.

When Hannah is selected for a high level post with the United Nations High Commission for Refugees, she finds herself in a dilemma. Her excitement at the opportunities that open up before her, her elation at being chosen, are overshadowed by the difficult necessity of telling Sonny. But she is aware of the inevitability of change that the law of life between man and woman, the law of love, has to obey the other law of life—moving on. "How would change come, for her, if she stayed on in the cottage, conveniently near for visits from Sonny?" Hannah is too honest and open to ever want Sonny to leave Aila and his family, her "romantic respect" for his family dictates this. She also knows that change has crept into their relationship.

When Aila is arrested, Hannah is the one who finds out where she is being held and manages to get a note from Sonny smuggled to her. But her concern for Aila is both a source of comfort to Sonny and a painful reminder of her life outside their personal relationship. When she lies beside him, he seems to see her as if in her professional capacity, as she had been earlier, visiting him in prison, writing him morale-building letters. And when she says: "I'll be able to come back sometimes," he feels a sense of betrayal and a line from Shakespeare's *Othello* surfaces in his mind: "Oh thou weed: who art so lovely faire, and smell'st so sweet that the sense aches at thee, Would thou had'st never been born."

Much of what we know about Hannah comes from what Will, the adolescent son, tells us. His point of view is skewed by the hostility he feels towards this intruder in their family, and by the special protectiveness and concern he feels towards his mother whose place is threatened by Hannah. Hatred and disgust govern his feelings for "that woman with her bare pink bottle-calves and clumsy sandals," whom he sees coming out of the cinema with his father, and whose dress when she had come to their house during his father's prison term, consisted of an embroidered blouse with a long denim skirt with guerilla military pockets, so that Will, remembering the occasion, thinks sarcastically, "couldn't she make up her mind whether she wanted to look as if she'd just come from a garden party or a Freedom Fighter's hide in the bush?" (9) But her blurred, undefined features are set off by blue eyes "like the dabs filled in with brilliant colour in an otherwise unfinished sketch." To Will, however, she is only a "clumsy blonde," "pudding-faced" like pink blancmange, with the "show-off picture on the wall" who reminds him of pig when he notices "A few bright hairs [which] look like filaments of glass embedded in the pink flesh round her mouth."

In the character of Hannah we see reflected Gordimer's despair at the way apartheid brings about a rift in even the most meaningful relationships, an unbridgeable divide between black and white.

Hannah's simplicity, sincerity and devotion to duty shine out in the novel. Her desire to help those oppressed by unjust state laws is genuine. In Sonny, she finds a soulmate and companion and her pleasure in their relationship stems as much from sexual fulfillment as from bonding with a partner in the political struggle. She is generous enough to accept Aila's superior rights in the relationship and no thought of replacing her or of breaking up the family ever enters her mind. She is a constant support for them, soothing Baby when she breaks down in court and searching out information about where Aila is being held. She sees through the dangers of Sonny's 'trusting idealism' and how it blinds him to the harsh realities of their situation. As

Sonny falls in importance and political flavour, and as he goes through the shock of Aila's abandonment, he indirectly blames Hannah: "O thou weed . . ." However, Hannah's honesty and dedication makes her put duty above self despite the pain it causes her. She is more pragmatic in her acceptance of the law that life has to move on.

Baby

Will's little sister and Sonny's precious daughter, Baby enjoys the happy childhood that Aila and Sonny create for their children, learning useful activities like dress-making from her mother and joining the Junior Red Cross. She is called "bright little madam" by everyone, with none of the intellectual interests that Sonny tries to instil in his children, a girl who would rather listen to her little radio than read or be read to by her father. Yet, she is Sonny's favourite child, "his darling," "his beauty," and as Hannah notices, a girl in whom the mother's beauty was reproduced as "pert prettiness." (62)

Baby displays no interest in the political happenings in the outside world, and is absorbed in her dancing lessons, pop-star worship and bosom friendships. Thus it comes as a shock to the whole family when she cuts her wrists in an attempted suicide, during a party at a friend's place. Sonny is not at home at the time. The doctor tells Aila that it was evident to him that Baby took drugs and that her great liveliness was deep unhappiness. Both Will and his mother now know that Baby, too, knows about Sonny's affair, it was just that she has managed her knowledge differently. "The hip, hyped style she flaunted on street corners (out of sight of my mother; I saw her), the flip and vulgar way she

. . . talked; the emotional outbursts over trifles, that my mother put down to the strain of having had my father in detention and on trial during the time when her menstrual cycle was being established, her manner of distancing herself from the childhood she and I had in common—all these were her attempts to manage." (42)

Though she recovers and appears outwardly to be unaffected by her experience, wearing brightly painted wooden bracelets on her wrists, frizzing her beautiful straight shining hair, going around the house with one of Will's old shirts tied under her naked breasts, midriff showing, moving her hips to music from her Walkman—there is a change in her that Will senses. As she casually tries to explain to him the circumstances that lead her to try and kill herself, Will sees that she is putting up a performance, trying to hide the real reasons behind her trauma, and that the real reason is their father's betrayal of faith. Yet, close as she is to her father, she tries to warn Will off from involvement in his personal life. This angers Will. He feels she is covering up for him and in a way encouraging him—"although she looks like my mother, she's devious and lying as he is." (55)

Baby takes up a job with an insurance agent and lives away from home, but she comes whenever it suits her, bringing flowers or a ripped hem for Aila to mend, hooking an arm round her father and kissing his ear, if he is there. Coquetry is inborn in her, even when she is addressing her father. She is pretty, talkative and amusing, mimicking and laughing and begging for gossip about family and friends, whom, Will notices, she never sees any more. And most of all, he notices her vulgarity, though Aila tries to excuse her: "As long as Baby's busy and happy," she says.

When Baby suddenly announces that she is going away to join the resistance, it is a matter of pride and even excitement for Sonny. He arrogantly assumes that he is in a better position to cope with the loss of a daughter because of his political commitment, while for Aila, because she is a stay-at-home wife, all is loss. So his discomfiture is all the more keen when he comes to know that Aila has managed to get a passport and visa to visit Baby in Lusaka.

Aila comes back full of news about Baby. She is married, expecting a child, she has planted a garden with herbs. Aila travels back and forth, ostensibly to be with Baby during her pregnancy and childbirth, and this provides her with the perfect cover for the resistance activities which Aila also gets involved in. Sonny comes to know of this much later, but through Aila he comes to know of the dangerous and unsettled lives led by young freedom fighters like Baby and her husband, who have to take their little child along with them to meetings and parties because it was unsafe to leave the little one at home where a bomb could go off any time.

Thus, Baby comes to represent the hidden strength of the ordinary people in the struggle, whose outwardly cheap appearance and apparently unmotivated lives, conceals unguessed-at commitment, and Will feels that he would, some day, want to tell everybody their story.

NOTE

1. Nadine Gordimer, *My Son's Story* (Delhi: Doaba, 2001).

My Son's Story: The Political Background

My Son's Story is set in the turbulent period of the 70s which were prefaced by the equally turbulent years of the 60s, in which the ANC and the PAC, prohibited from operating peacefully or even having a legal existence in South Africa, established underground organizations to carry out their struggle against the government.[1] The militant wing of the ANC (Umkhonto we-Sizwe—the Spear of the Nation) targeted strategic places such as police stations and power plants. Poqo (Blacks Only) the militant wing of the PAC also engaged in the campaign of terror. Some young white students and professionals established their own organization, the anti-apartheid African Resistance Movement and carried out bomb attacks.

But by 1964, the police had succeeded in crushing all these movements. The Group Areas Act led to forcible relocation of the black and further repression. With the ANC and PAC banned, African university students decided to form a movement of their own. Led by Steve Biko, an African medical student at the University of Natal, they established the South African Students' Organization in 1969. Biko argued that blacks often suppressed themselves by accepting their second class status accorded to them by the apartheid system and he stressed that they had to liberate themselves mentally as well as physically. In the novel, Biko's work is one of the books that Sonny possesses.

SASO expanded enormously and its members established black self-help projects, including workshops and medical clinics.

In 1974, the government decided to enforce the Bantu Education Act that required Afrikaans to be used on an equal basis with English as a medium of instruction because Afrikaans was identified by Africans, especially by the young as the language of the oppressor, opposition to this new policy grew through 1975 and 1976. Students's organizations began to boycott classes.

On June 16, 1976, hundreds of high school students in Soweto, south west of Johannesburg, marched in protest against having to use Afrikaans. The police responded with tear gas and then with gun fire that left 3 dead and a dozen injured. Clashes between the demonstrators and the police cost several hundred African lives. SASO and BPC were banned and open black resistance was brought to a halt.

By the middle of the 1970s, apartheid was clearly under strain. The popularity of Black Consciousness and the massive levels of participation in the Soweto demonstrations illustrated profound discontent among the black population, particularly the young and an increasing readiness to challenge the system physically. Hundreds of young Africans slipped across South Africa's northern borders in the aftermath of Soweto and volunteered to fight as guerilla soldiers for the PAC and the ANC. In the novel, Baby's decision to join the military wing of the resistance and later Aila's role as a secret member of the revolutionary organization, very clearly belongs to this phase of apartheid history. Aila is accused of being a member of an organization called the Transvaal Implementation Machinery, responsible for acts of terrorism in the region and connected to a high command named Amos Sebokeng. She is also accused of having acted as a courier between Umkhonto weSizwe in neighbouring countries and a cell in the Johannesburg area, to have attended meetings where missions for the placing of explosives were planned and to have illegally concealed terrorist arms in her home. The leaders of the movement arrange for her defence, but later find it advisable that she entreat bail and leave the country. Her supporters speak of putting her case before human rights organizations like Amnesty International.

In the late 1970s, some of these people began to re-enter South Africa secretly to carry out sabotage attacks on various targets that were seen as symbols of apartheid. Meanwhile neighbouring countries like Angola, Mozambique and Rhodesia (Zimbabwe) attained independence and there were growing anti-apartheid sentiments in Britain and Europe. In 1973, the United Nations declared apartheid "a crime against humanity" and in 1977 declared mandatory the existing embargo on the sale of arms to South Africa. Thus, in the novel, the character of Hannah, as representative of a human rights organization and later her selection to an important post in the United Nations, is completely credible.

Apartheid permeates Sonny and Aila's life so completely that they almost come to see it as part of the nature of things. Segregation dictates that the blacks live in special areas designated for them, from which they are only allowed to emerge on Saturdays to shop in the cheapest stores and queue up in lines separated from where the whites are served. Cinemas are out of bounds for them as is the tea room and the library, as well as the seaside hotels, beaches and pleasure grounds with swimming pools; and though the department store has a cloakroom for the use of white customers, the blacks have to make do with the toilets in the railway station, the only ones provided for their kind. Though there are not many notices spelling out this demarcation, except on the public benches, the lines are clearly drawn. "As some lordly wild animal marks the boundaries of his hunting and mating ground which no other may cross, it was as if the municipality left some warning odour, scent of immutable authority, where the Saturday people were not to transgress." (7) Cultural societies like the music society or the Sunday bird-watchers' group or chess club exclude blacks like Sonny who would want to enrich their minds. Apart from the constant humiliations and slights that pressed on him the moment he ventured outside his community, Sonny experiences discrimination at a more personal level: the people of his community were underpaid; as an adult, he earned less than a white teacher with the same level of qualification.

The atmosphere is full of hope, though, as well as skepticism about these hopes: "they going to get a rope round their necks that what they putting up their hands for, bracelets man bullets up the backside you can't win against whitey." (15) Sonny follows political trials in the newspapers, and has read a copy of the charter that had come out of "a great meeting" (the Congress of the People) and that you could go to prison for possessing. But the catalyst for the beginnings of Sonny's involvement in politics comes in the aftermath of the Education Act, with the schools in turmoil and the school children boycotting classes. He leads the children in their march across the veldt to show solidarity with the children who has been locked out of school by the police after one such boycott. His name enters police files after he searches in police stations for children arrested for arson.

The forcible relocation of black people with government trucks carting away people and their possessions and by bulldozers pushing over what had been their homes, becomes a horrifying reality. Shopkeepers who were not really black but not white either, were moved out of the shops they had occupied for generations in the white towns. The townships where the blacks are herded together were composed of breached walls and tottering fences which were one with the components—tin, hubcaps, rotting board—of rubbish mounds. The streets were gullies and also children's sandpits, fecal streams, the fodder-grounds of pigs, chickens and dogs. The air was overhung with the "acrid incense" of smoke. Sonny begins studying government white papers in the tin-trunk archives of township proclamations and his name starts to appear on posters announcing political meetings, "where they were scrawled over obscenely or torn down by local whites." And it becomes clear that "For them, their kind . . . there was only one meaning: the political struggle."

Sonny becomes the one sent to help people who lived in wretched conditions in the ghettos organize resident organizations; for rent boycotts, he would teach them how to organize the campaign; when miners, municipal workers or workers in a factory or brickyard went on strike, he is involved in their meetings and the tactics of other forms of resistance like stickers and T-shirts with slogans to be displayed until they provoked a ban.

The decision for him and his family to move in among the whites is part of the tactic of resistance to show the whites that segregation is unacceptable, and Sonny tells Aila in anger: "We don't have a vote for their council but they take our money for the privilege of living in this ghetto." (25) When Sonny is imprisoned, he enters a new world, of glass barriers behind which the prisoners were allowed to meet visitors, flanked by surly warders; the trials, where "the cheerful atmosphere of airport reunions at tea-break were the 'humanized' part of a process whose purpose was to send these men, who already had spent many months in detention, back to prison as convicts; part of the processing of all opposition to the State pulped into prison." (37) The people gathered to wines the trials of friends and relatives listen to a farcical process where "the sacrifice of their individual lives for man against evil slowly is distorted by the law in volumes of recorded words, police videos, in the mouths of State witnesses into an indictment for having committed evil." (61)

Sonny experiences first-hand the "bonding" of prison life, where the secret signs between the brotherhood are the messages tapped with a knuckle to be received by an ear pressed to the other side of a wall. The blood brotherhood is exchanged when hymns are taken up from cell to cell to accompany an unknown to the hangman, and then the warders come and kick the cell doors and swear.

Even after his release, he faces the ever-present police movie cameras, which await those who come out of political meetings, and knows that he is always being watched by the Security Police, an anonymous, unseen presence in his personal life, who hope that he might lead them to those of his underground associates still unknown to them.

The terrifying reality of state repression becomes evident during the incident of the graveyard ceremony for the nine young men, aged between fifteen and twenty-six, who have been killed in police action. As Hannah accompanies other white supporters in a combi which are used to transport blacks back and forth between township and city, she notices the electronically operated gates and spike and razor wire-topped walls that guard the park, meant for white only, from intrusion. The unarmed crowd at the meeting is surrounded by mounted police and soldiers with automatic shotguns and R4 rifles. "There was no getting away from them. They were life; and death." (76) Armoured vans and cars (which the people dub "Hippos"), with steel aerials are ranged around, and fierce Alsatian dogs tug at leashes held by police handlers. Yet, the atmosphere is one of determination with the people singing freedom songs and crying out "Amandla," "Viva." When the police lob tear gas shells into the crowd, the people pull out rags kept on their persons as protection against the fouled cloud as white people carry credit cards.

The political strategies include not only direct attack on the government, but also building up opposition to its policies, social, military and economic, throughout the world. Comrades who are arrested are immediately replaced by others ready to do their work, and this changing of leadership serves to defeat bans and imprisonments. With the endless disruption of a hounding State—files seized, offices burned down, comrades become nomads sleeping when and where they could, and, in the novel, this allows Sonny to carry on his affair with Hannah without difficulty, because everyone thought it natural that a man like him could not reveal his whereabouts to even his family for security reasons.

Even when the winds of factionalism blow over the organization, Sonny keeps himself busy with planning and running workshops—"resistance education" in shanties and mud churches, under the guise of local club meetings, since the National Education Crisis Committee was restricted by a ban. And it is in tune with the times that he finds a young man apparently a hitch-hiker, at Hannah's doorstep and senses that he is some kind of secret agent. The young man leaves as suddenly as he had come, discarding his hitch-hiker's outfit and Sonny senses that he must have changed persona for the next stage of his mission, especially when he finds an empty bottle of hair bleach in the bathroom.

The turbulence of black politics, where disaffection breeds cabals, requires the necessity of disciplining the separatist group, and though Sonny is not chosen for this, he is in caucus meetings with trade union leaders and a delegate to secret meetings with other affiliated radical groups, to discuss their support. Reports come in from those who are informers for the movement. Now the enemy was no longer definitively the government, the police, the army, but also one's own people. Terms are offered for the sake of unity and discussed. It is agreed that the men be suspended, not expelled.

Both Hannah and Sonny are concerned about the shape of the new future that awaits the country. The discussion between them highlights the opposition between socialist and left thinking, as Hannah puts it: "it's not so long since you learnt to change the idea you had of yourselves as powerless against whites. The old Left did it, by God! Thank God. Only the old Left." (148) For Sonny, the old structures are changing, so that now it is much more than a matter of being willing to die for one's freedom, it is a matter of feeding, housing and educating people, of giving generations of uprooted people and refugees somewhere to live. He feels that this aspect needs more attention than is being given, and that the old socialist models may have become obsolete, even though many would regard this as a betrayal. As he puts it: "I hope to god we're not going to cling to something that's had its day, when we take over. If the old socialism is dying, let's admit it and make sure we can find our liberation in the new Left that's coming." (149)

The ugly realities of a police state machinery become evident to Sonny and Will at a very personal level, when Aila is arrested for her revolutionary activities under the Internal Securities Act. They attend the hearing not at the city magistrate's courts in the district of the mining corporation's headquarters, where already an explosion had one day taken place, but in a court across the veldt in Soweto. Armoured vehicles, armed police, Black Marias from where prisoners are escorted in by warders, dragged, punched, shaken or shouted at, these are the sights that greet the visitors and Sonny has to divert the attention of a policeman by speaking in the idiom of prison Afrikaans as Will slips past with the lawyer.

Yet, it is this very environment that creates heroism in unexpected ways. As Hannah comes to realize: "To monitor trials is to 'monitor' the soaring graph of feelings that move men and women to act, endangering themselves; the curves and drops of bravery, loss of nerve, betrayal; cunning learned by courage, courage learned by discipline—and others which exceed the competence of any graph to record, would melt its needle in the heat of intensity: the record of people who, receiving a long jail sentence, tell the court they regret nothing; of those who, offered amnesty on condition that they accept this 'freedom' in place of the concept for which they went to prison, choose to live out their lives there. Such inconceivable decisions are beyond the capacity of anyone who does not make one. The spirit's shouldering of the world, as Atlas's muscles took on the physical weight of the world. Such people cannot be monitored." (61)

NOTE

1. Excerpted in part from Internet, Library of Congress Studies, http://cweb2loc.gov

My Son's Story: Reviews[1]

Laurel Graeber in *The New York Times*:

Much of the novel's power and interest derive from her [Nadine Gordimer's] almost uncanny ability to portray each of the novel's characters with sympathy and subtlety. "The book is really about the problems the ordinary forms of love bring within a particular context" said Miss Gordimer, "in which love of country is inextricably bound up with these other types of love. And by love of country, I don't mean gung-ho patriotism, but involvement with the time."

Ravonne A. Green in *Publisher's Weekly*:

Highly praised as a literate goad to South Africa's conscience under apartheid, Gordimer here delivers her most perceptive and powerful novel in years. The story of a man's evolution as a political activist and the toll it takes on his family and on him, it is also a picture of a marriage and an extra-marital affair, set against the backdrop of daily life in segregated South Africa, even as the winds of change begin to blow. An exemplary husband and father, a pillar of rectitude in the black community, Sonny is dismissed from his teaching job after he leads a political protest. On his release from his imprisonment, he becomes a leader in the revolutionary underground; at the same time he is swept into an affair with a white woman, a worker in a human rights organization. The intertwined events that lead to the break-up of Sonny's family and the tragic end of his high hopes and ideal are partially narrated by his teenaged son Will, bitter and cynical over his father's betrayal. The novel is eloquent in its understanding of moral complexities in a land where blacks keep rags on their persons as protection against tear gas "as whites people carry credit cards." Tightly focused and controlled, expertly plotted, the narrative is replete with ironies; the tension increases almost invisibly, until the unexpected, jolting denouement. In the end, Will resolves to record "what it really was like to live a life determined by the struggle to be free, as desert dwellers' days are determined by the struggle against thirst and those of dwellers amid snow and ice by the struggle against the numbing of cold," which is exactly what this book does, honestly and memorably.

Elise Chase in *Forbes Library*:

Gordimer's new novel, about a coloured South African family ravaged by the father's affair with a white human rights advocate, probes with breathtaking power and precision the complexities of "love, love/hate" and the interplay of public and private reality. First person narration shows Will's struggle to deal with confusion and bitterness after discovering Sonny's infidelity. Alternating third person sequences depict Sonny's evolution from committed school teacher and devoted husband/father into a resistance worker for whom the movement itself ultimately becomes a second family—one his loyal wife Aila cannot share with him, though his lover Hannah does. Gordimer retains perfect control over her material, rendering her characters' shifting perspectives with truly extraordinary empathy and discernment.

Andrew Sullivan in *The New York Times*, Dec. 2001:

It's extremely hard to write beautifully about the power of sex, of its capacity to elevate humans out of worlds that would divide them, of its occasionally transcendent quality. But Gordimer writes elegantly about it so easily we barely notice the accomplishment.

Bruce King in *World Literature in Review*, ed. Pamela A. Genova (Gale, 2003), p. 1602:

In Nadine Gordimer's novels the personal, especially the psychological and moral, intersects with and is influenced by the political. In a society so politicized the relation of the individual to the social world becomes political, and morality finds expression in terms of ideology and commitment. However, the strength of the novels has been their focus on the individual and on families and their awareness of the personal complexities, compulsions and ironies that are the sources of political consciousness and decisions. *My Son's Story* makes the poetics of Gordimer's novels too explicit and seems too diagrammatic. It is almost as if she were explaining her fiction while showing how it can take new directions appropriate to a future South Africa. Perhaps the most difficult novel she has attempted, and filled with her personal obsessions found in previous novels . . . it often feels contrived, manipulated, abstract, programmatic. Too many sentences seem to be the author speaking through the narrator.

My Son's Story is an uncomfortable novel to read for the story is told by the jealous son of a black African revolutionary hero. The son is the supposed author of the novel, which is in part his maturation from jealous youth concerned about family loyalties to an adult who now perceives his family's actions as a heroic response to the political demands made upon the gifted by the times. The same values that made them a family make them into moral beings. There is an oppressiveness in reading of the son's sexual jealousy caused by his father's mistress (a blonde white woman), the son's resentment of his father's emotional withdrawal from the family due to total involvement in the movement and his mistress, the son's perception of his father's example as being the reason for his sister's going into exile in order to work for the movement and for his mother's eventual politicization, hiding weapons, and escape into exile. The story of the fragmentation of a black family due to politics becomes, as the son writes the novel, the story of exemplary heroism and of how life is changed by external circumstances so that the personal is given its direction by the political.

Gordimer's attempt to write about black African lives is itself a way to cross the colour line, a way to claim a place in the future black-ruled South Africa. The mother even matures from passive wife to female African hero. However, the conquering of new fictional spaces has its costs. There is, no doubt consciously, none of the detailed specificity of social life, the art objects, the houses, the background, the complexities of characterization found in Gordimer's portraits of white characters elsewhere. Too much is avoided or left unknowable. There is also none of the imagining, the fantasies, the desires in conflict presented fully, of the previous fiction. It is as if she were unable to enter, or out of political correctness refrained from fully entering, the minds of her characters. Instead conflicts are explicitly stated, and we are told how to interpret. This can be blamed on the narrator; it is his first novel, and we are told that he is writing a history of his family as an example of the personal costs of the black revolution; but the self-reflectivity of the fiction is not really a justification for turning the personal into the heroic, for the predictable way each character dedicated him or herself to the movement, or for the continual pointing to the themes by the narrator or author. Perhaps, as the ironies become clearer, *My Son's Story* will wear better on further readings.

NOTE

1. From internet http://www.nybooks.com/authors/629 and Barnesandnoble.comllc

My Son's Story: Themes and Issues

Broadly speaking, Nadine Gordimer's work focuses on the human tensions generated by apartheid. She is interested in what history does to particular people. She feels that even the most private selves, in the most private situations are "What they are because their lives are regulated and their mores formed by the political situation. You see, in South Africa, society is the political situation."[1]

Her earlier fiction had thrown a searchlight on the roles and choices open to whites in a segregated society, but in her later work, the struggle and impetus for change is clearly in the hands of the blacks and her investigation focuses on how this leads to a changed perspective in both. As she says in the Salon interview: "Mostly I am interviewed by white people and identified with white society. Hardly anybody says to me, "How are blacks dealing with change?" They're only interested in how whites are. And after all, whites are a minority. There are huge changes in the lives of blacks as well and even though one would think this is just release and freedom, it brings its problems."[2] The problems are basically the same—how to measure up in one's daily, personal life to one's avowed ethical and political principles, how to balance commitments to one's family with the heavy demands of political activism, given the temptations of private pleasure—not only sex, but the addictions of celebrity and power.

These problems are at the core of novels like *My Son's Story* and *None to Accompany Me* where the focus is on conflicting loyalties, the difficult terrain where personal interests, desires and ambitions encounter the demands and trials of a politically active life. Gordimer sees that the fight for freedom can have unanticipated consequences. A frequent theme is the pursuit of happiness for the individual in conflict with his or her duties to society. Gordimer concentrates on the failure of relationships due to these conflicts, on both sides of the colour bar and the recognition of isolation which comes to those who fail.

My Son's Story is set at the point where the personal intersects the political. This is the inevitable consequence of life in a country like South Africa, where the personal cannot be separated from the political. As Gordimer herself says: "the creative imagination, whatever it seizes upon, finds the focus of even the most private event set in the overall social determination of racial laws."

As the title of the novel suggests, this is a story of a father and a son..In this context, what Gordimer herself has to say about the relationship between parents and children is significant: "There is one common experience most of us have: we have been children and have suffered from our parents' not understanding us—and indeed, they didn't. Then the position is reversed, and you are the parent, and so you occupy both roles in your life. I think they are both mysterious and I have been exploring this my whole life—you don't ever really know anybody completely. A person, a persona, is made up of many different views and experiences of that person's life. It is not only your experience, it is also how others experience you."[3] Thus a central idea in this work is that of the inconsistencies of human behaviour, the many and disparate truths about human experience, its troubling contradictions and paradoxes.

My Son's Story is a novel about love, family and marriage in the context of the post Soweto society of segregated South Africa in the 70s, and so, it is both a story of domestic manners (the triangle of two women and a man, or of father, mother and son) and a political novel of contemporary urban South Africa, where the struggle for freedom has intensified into open defiance and underground resistance, even though some of the barriers have been ostensibly reduced to create an impression of liberalization, so that cinema halls and resorts are now open to blacks and interracial sex is no longer outlawed.

The theme of relationships that take on an unusual colouring from the particular circumstances that are their source is linked to the theme of commitment—personal and political. In fact, it is the commitment initially to family that broadens out into a concern for society at large and an involvement with the movement for its freedom and integrity that sets in motion the chain of events that lead to the tragic break up of Sonny's life. In the beginning, Sonny is the honourable, loving father and husband committed to his family despite the terrible shadow of apartheid. Sonny's care for his immediate family—Aila, Will and Baby—the "charmed circle" that he draws around them is an expression of his distinction that marks him out from the rest of his people. He passes on to Aila his desire to live usefully, not only for one's children, relatives or even one's own self, but with a sense of responsibility towards the community at large. Thus, Sonny keeps away from the evils of drugs, lackeyism, corruption and nepotism that drag down others of his kind. There are no beer or brandy bottles or loud music in his yard, rather he cultivates his appreciation of literature, takes courses to improve his mind, throws himself energetically into community activities and encourages his children in meaningful activities meant to broaden their minds. His idea of bettering himself was to study for a higher qualification, which he felt would be more useful in the long run. Initially, Sonny resists being drawn into the movement, so that he is dismissed as useless, a sell-out, "interested in getting some piddling bit of paper that would make him the paid agent of hand-out education" by those who are already involved.

But as his skills as a speaker lead him away from the small world of school-teaching, into the turbulent world of the political struggle, where his profession now becomes meetings, campaigns, the delegations to the authorities, it is the beginning of tragedy. The personal commitment to family, which had made him "whole," now experiences a disjunction. His political commitments inevitably lead to a prison sentence and to Hannah, the white human rights activist who monitors political trials. In Hannah he sees a comrade who 'like him' has given herself to the cause. Through her, he comes to inhabit a world where there is more than just "family affairs" to engage his attention, where "sexual happiness and political commitment were one" (86) and where "because it was all one, in them, they turned from caresses to worried discussion about the action of police agents provocateurs among church groups in rent boycotts." (57). But in trying to gain a whole new world, Sonny jeopardizes his own world.

Caught up in the thrilling experience of political struggle that Sonny comes to know at first hand after his prison sentence, he feels that his political commitment has given him emotions which, changed by harsh circumstance, enables him to deal with a whole order of situations not accounted for in family affairs. He believes that because Hannah was not like any other woman, their relationship was formed "in a special and different morality: the excruciating recasting of the meaning of love." (87) What he does not see is that the old morality still ties him down, so that his relationship with Hannah is interpreted by his son Will as a betrayal of the code of self-respect that Sonny had upheld and instilled in his family. Will's perplexity, anger, bitterness and frustration is expressed with great vehemence and it changes slowly to a withering scorn. His sarcasm forces us to look at moral complexity, moral ambiguity, moral hypocrisy.

The betrayal of established principles governing the relationship between a parent and child, when Sonny forces an outraged Will into unwilling complicity with his extramarital affair, is also the beginning of tragic error of judgment. Sonny complacently assumes that because Will does not mention his meeting his father with Hannah at the cinema, "It's as if it never happened." (50) Sonny's relationship with Hannah is also a betrayal of the marriage tie. Will senses that Sonny's feelings of having left Aila behind as being just a stay-at-home wife without any understanding of the larger issues contributes to his confidence in indulging in an affair. "What I'd like to know," asks Will indignantly, "is does prison give my father the freedom to do what he's doing. Is it all right so long as she doesn't know.

That is what he was getting me to agree to when he made me look at him across the table that night after the cinema." (30)

The distance between Sonny and Aila in their personal relationship widens because he sees a sameness in her that does not satisfy him any longer; Aila did not seem to catch on to the trick of using private, oblique language as a code to bypass the watchful eyes of prison warders. The usual talk of family matters turns into silences without communication of any kind. "Why did Aila never speak? Why did she never say what he wanted her to say?" (39) Sonny's growing unconcern with family matters blinds him to the value of Aila's quiet strength and her determination to carry on bravely even in the face of adversity. This translates itself into apparently simple things like dressing with great care and elegance even when visiting Sonny in prison or bringing him clothes fresh from the dry cleaners and keeping a carry-all packed at all times, with the necessities for maintaining cleanliness, so that Sonny could have the means of self-respect so important to him. "The pullover is her means of love," Will says perceptively. (83)

With Hannah, Sonny experiences the joy of making love to someone who, too, is in the battle "for whom the people in the battle are her only family, her life, the happiness she understands." (46) He experiences the sense of "erotic fun" as he had never experienced it before: "To leave, separately, a gathering where each had given full attention to serious decisions . . . and fifteen minutes later be undressing each other: what an exquisite range of changing responses such an afternoon expanded." (48) As she becomes "a euphoria natural as a pulse beat with him wherever he went," he becomes more and more adept at deceiving and more and more oblivious to his personal commitments: "And every now and then, in the carefully arranged and guarded life he was managing, when he judged it was time to approach Aila again—to pretend to want poor Aila, oh my god—the act drained him, in shame. Sometimes, he felt a final spurt of anger, towards Aila, sperm turned to venom." (47)

But Sonny does not realize that this relationship which apparently was superior to, and an escape from, the daily deadened state of marriage, and which had brought him such supreme happiness, was, in fact an escape from all other claims on him; that "the physical illusion of personal freedom" would fade "as the lulled and sated senses come back and relay the knowledge of time passing with traffic: work, loss, hunger and pain, pacing out there in the street: other people" (48); that the very intensity of the experience made it inevitable that it could not last.

His obtuseness comes home to him in a most horrifying way when he returns to find that his daughter had attempted suicide. Though Sonny knows that something had driven her to it, he does not make any serious attempt to find out; in fact, the only thing he can find to say is: Will there be scars? He takes the easy way out by discussing what Baby could do in the future. As Will says ironically: "All was resolved as a matter of the right occupation." (53) And again: "He was able to forget so quickly." (55) When Baby decides to leave home and join the military wing of the resistance movement, Sonny sees great sorrow in Aila's face and knows he is responsible for her pain, but he cannot stop himself from feeling excitement and pride. And once again, his arrogance surfaces: "His Baby was not the dainty little daughter of a schoolteacher now. Aila must realize they were not living humbly in their designated place outside Benoni." (86)

But the taint that has seeped into Sonny's personal relationships has its unforeseeable effect on his political commitment. The cleansing of the graves ceremony sees Sonny deliver a powerful speech full of references to freedom, democracy, peace and justice. Yet, when the police lob tear gas shells at the crowd and cause a stampede, that later leads to firing, Sonny runs with Hannah "as if he were chained to her." A young man falls face down in their path. Instinctively obedient to instilled principles, the old Benoni ghetto avowals, Sonny turns back to lift him, even as he sees Father Mayekiso bend over the dead man, forgetful of personal danger. But at that very moment a bullet grazes past Hannah's head and, forgetful of his old principles of usefulness and responsibility, of not living for oneself, he runs to save Hannah and himself. "Now he had something he would never speak, not to anyone." (87) But Hannah knows the truth that eludes Sonny: "you don't live for each other, the loving is contained within the cause, and there would be no love if you were to refuse, because of personal risk, something expected of you by the struggle." (121)

Sonny's betrayal is tragically out of character, but it is a deed that is irreversible: "However well a human being is known, it is never known what is moving in him towards a decisive act, something 'out of character,' it's not to be seen how it is slowly coming about, what is preparing for it, the turning aside, the betrayal. You run away and leave the dying man. Just once." (126) With this betrayal of principles comes a sense of isolation: "A rich white man's domain of quiet and beauty screened by green from screams of fear and chants of rage, from the filth of scrap heap settlements and the smashed symmetry of shot bodies; he had no part in it." (99)

Though Sonny justifies his relationship with Hannah as being part of a "man's responsibility for loving, inside or outside conventional morality," and believes that his "capacity for living fully" made him equal to all the demands made on him—"dedication to liberation, maintenance of family, private passion" (157) and also that, since he had even given his daughter for liberation, nothing could be seen to deflect his attention from the struggle, he gives himself away when he looks for ways and means to get the order against Hannah's re-entry into the country rescinded. He explains to himself that he is doing it because she is "invaluable" but the selfish personal motive is too strong to suppress. It is clear that his commitment has been deflected, no matter how he tries to justify it to himself.

Educated as he is in the tactics of the political struggle, Sonny knows that he has allowed himself to become a target for blackmail by the Security Police, the "dread barter" of "we'll detain her for the political confidences you've made to her, unless you give us some confidences." (112) He also knows that he is now marked out as less than totally committed and therefore, less trustworthy, so that he is visited in secret by a group of men who seek to form a cabal to oust certain leaders.

Gordimer's major theme—that of the tragic undercurrents that sully the personal relationships of people whose lives are devoted to the cause, the all-too-human conceits and deceits that taint their basic goodness, dignity and courage—is developed at this point in the story, which charts the downfall of Sonny. Even as he tries to convince himself that he was not a lover in the conventional sense, that "Revolutionaries, activists, are whole men and women; only human. Such marginal encounters have nothing to do with dedication and dependability," (131) he knows that he has been labelled 'unreliable' and that a shadow had been cast from Hannah.

The tragedy of apartheid that casts its shadow on even the most well meaning of individuals is the fate of Sonny's relationship with a white woman that has made him open to suspicion and jeopardized his political career. He has regarded Hannah as "one of themselves, in a way. . . . But only in a way; not directly in the movement, certainly not acceptable as party to deliberations, decisions and tactics, and therefore not—most important—subject to discipline. He knew that. Sonny, who had been the most disciplined of men, knew that about her, however close he allowed her to come. And to come close to him was to come close to the movement. He knew he was responsible for that; and of course he was aware they knew it." (132) The divide between black and white remains unbridgeable.

Though Sonny is reinstated, he loses his key position. He sees with anguish and self-pity, all his sacrifices washed away, the fact that he had abandoned a career he loved, given up the forming of minds of a future generation for the uncertain reputation of a popular platform demagogue, left the cosy circle of family for the existence under surveillance, the prison cell. He thinks of the unspoken criticism being levelled against him: "And do you remember, that time . . . the business of the cabal. . . . And that other time, before, the cleansing of the graves . . . his big speech, and then." (139) What he has lost is, tragically, what he most valued in himself—his trust in himself.

But what he only vaguely realizes is that he has compromised his allegiance to the party on the ground that the party owed him something, for Sonny become "Sonny." It is this "hubris" that leads to disaster. The exhilaration of being at the centre of the struggle brings its own specious self-justifications, but in the end, the realities are different. Now it is Aila who is in the centre of the resistance movement, and Sonny experiences a dire displacement. The core of life, which he had thought lay with Hannah, in reality belongs to his life with Aila. Because of Hannah, Aila was gone. She whom he had always regarded as "poor Aila" was the revolutionary now.

The epigraph of *My Son's Story* ("You had a Father, let your son say so") taken from Shakespeare's sonnet, points to the other major theme of the novel—the relationship between a father and a son, one which, as Will is to tell us later, consists of both love and love/hate. Will is the author of the story which is "ours. My father's and mine," (193) and as the title suggests, he imagines the pride with which his father introduces his work, "my son's story," for it is a fulfillment of an old ambition, to see his son becoming a writer. But this writing has come about at great cost, through the pain of the destruction of a familiar way of life.

The structure of the narrative, with the objective, third person voice being interspersed with the subjective one ("Sometimes memory has opened a trapdoor and dropped me back into the experience as if I were living it again just at the stage I was when I lived it, so I've told it that way, in the present tense, with the vocabulary that was all I had to express myself, then"), provides a constant interplay of perspectives that allow the reader to assess the characters, even the flawed point of view of Will himself as narrator. This is in consonance with Gordimer's avowed interest, "all my life," in the "oblique picture of the narrator himself, emerging from the story he tells and the way he tells it; an unconscious revelation"[4]

It is thus, a novel about growth, for Will's experiences teach him about life at the personal and political levels in a way that would not have been granted to him without his involvement in Sonny's affair. He sees an idol having clay feet, he sees an ideal being betrayed, he learns about human weakness and failure, but he also learns about devotion, commitment and courage. He learns to overcome an attitude that is judgemental, full of resentment and self-pity, and to balance blame with praise. He also comes to realize that there are different kinds of heroism, that the obvious ones are not the only ones worth valuing. The rage that he had felt all along at being marginalized by both Sonny and Aila, who through their deception or protectiveness had kept him apart from the turbulence and dangers of political involvement, is exorcized through his writing. His role is that of a recorder, a witness: "I have that within that passeth show." The poem which he writes for his father is an acceptance of the harsh realities of life within the prison-like conditions of apartheid, where "lover, comrade, friend, child" or the bird of peace are all crushed "Against stone walls."

Commenting on Gordimer's narrative technique, Rowland Smith writes: "Gordimer's later work shows an increasingly confident use of fictional form. Not only does her political emphasis become more radical from the seventies on, but her controlled variations of point of view and narrative voice also combine with structural leitmotifs in language, image and metaphor to give her later novels extraordinary depth and resonance.

"Throughout her career Gordimer has insisted on the 'truth' or at least truthfulness, of her fiction. In a celebrated public address, she argued: 'I remain a writer, not a public speaker; nothing I say here will be as true as my fiction.' The consequences of this conviction is that she attempts in all her work to present the many-sidedness of the social and political situations she examines. Judgements by the reader emerge from the often-neutral presentation of events by the narrative voice. All the sides of the case have to be presented or at least alluded to. The inappropriateness of some attitudes, beliefs or behaviour informs the judgements implicit in the text, but seldom are the appropriate reactions spelled out by the author. In Gordimer's view, it is in the accuracy of her presentation and in the depth of her imaginative grasp of the events portrayed that the fictional 'truth' is to be found."[5] Gordimer's narrative technique in *My Son's Story* is geared to achieve just this—the truth about the tragic consequences of apartheid in the most intimate of personal relationships.

NOTES

1. Qtd. James Vinson, *Contemporary Novelists* (2nd ed., St. James Press, London, 1976), p. 543.

2. See Nadine Gordimer site http://dir.salon.com/books/int/1998/03/ 09.
3. From A Conversation with Nadine Gordimer by Donald Paul, <nttp://www.worcesterphoenix.com/archive/books/98/01/02/The_House_Gun_Barhtml>
4. Quoted in *World Literature Criticism Supplement,* Vol.1, Gale, 1997, p. 384.
5. From Lillian S. Robinson, ed., *Modern Women Writers* (Continuum, 1996), p. 202.

Treatment of Cross-Racial Relationship in Nadine Gordimer's *My Son's Story*

SUREKHA DANGWAL
H.N.B. Garhwal University, Srinagar-Garhwal

African writing, in its modern sense, began in the 18th century and developed inevitably as a protest literature. The primary impetus was derived from the dehumanizing institution of slavery. Whether he is African or American by place of birth, the black writer, by the condition of his existence, has been made intensely aware of a white civilization which, whatever its virtues, nevertheless does impose its domination on the black mind and body. This domination may be of the openly aggressive sort, such as the jailing of black leaders or the socio-economic imprisonment of black people in ghettos, or it may be of the covert sort whereby values accepted by whites are invoked by them in opposition to important black values.

Since modern African literature has developed out of the colonial experience, it is sometimes wrongly assumed that generalization can be applied to the entire continent without taking into account the different cultural, historical and social background to each nation's writing. Such generalizations ignore the relative ability or inability of different tribal cultures to sustain and survive the colonial experience. Each region of Africa has had a different historical experience and this is reflected in the variety of literary models and themes. The literature of English-speaking Africa is independent of European intellectual movements. In English-speaking West Africa, where there was no settler class and independence was gained early, there is little explicit political protest in literature beyond the pan-African militancy found in Ghana. South Africa, on the other hand, has a long history of foreign occupation, settlement and urbanization which has resulted in de-tribalisation of the Africans. This led to a literature of protesting inequality and discrimination under apartheid rather than a literature about African values:

> Even at its most militant, black South African writing is basically liberal in lamenting the loss of an integrated multiracial society. In South Africa the socio-political life presents the kind of challenge that produces writers.[1]

The colonial experience of South Africa has produced a large volume of verse and prose which portrays these relationships and in which the black man has to give an account of what the white man has done to him. There is a direct relation between the political perspective and literary creation in South Africa. In this relation the political perspective has tended to dominate. South African literature in English begins, as does the literature of Canada, Australia and the United States.

The white writers of South Africa who are internationally known are Jack Cope, Dan Jacobson, Olive Schreiner, Doris Lessing and Nadine Gordimer. When these writers refer to black protagonist, they do so as outsiders with an even more limited knowledge of the native's everyday experience than the black writers have. But the black writers are always between "The fear of expression and the need to give expression."[2]

As a native-born South African, Gordimer elected to stay in a country ruled by a single political party, whose policies shattered all her beliefs and feelings, and she experienced the consequences of that choice. A lifelong interest in politics led Gordimer through modifications of an essentially liberal and leftist position. When the Black consciousness movement rejected the involvement of whites, she registered her reaction in the essay "Where Do Whites Fit In?" While she has always publicly denied any political ideology, she today describes herself as "socialist" in outlook.

Apartheid has been her main subject throughout her career. She explored not merely its cruelty and dehumanizing effects on blacks, but also the costs of that cruelty and dehumanizing for the whites who superficially benefitted from it by law. She also examined the negative effects of apartheid even on those who opposed it, such as white liberals, who dedicated themselves for the cause of blacks, the whites revolutionaries, who gave their lives to this mission. Apartheid has provided so much material for her fiction that cross-racial relationship becomes the main theme of most of her stories. While Gordimer has brilliantly mastered the short story, her novels, given the greater scope of the novel form, stand out for their exploration of life in South Africa in particular and in newly emerging African nations in general. Her first three novels and her early short stories document the inception and early years of apartheid. The works explore the insidious effects of an ideology grounded exclusively in skin colour and demonstrate its impact on all South Africans In these texts we experience the traditional relationship between Prospero and Caliban in the acceptance within the European world and the native African margin. The idea of returning to England also finds open expression in the early works of Gordimer.

Gordimer has described herself as a "romantic struggling with reality."[3] And it is Gordimer the romantic who is aware of western man's longing to soil beyond the ambit of his own world, beyond his conscious identity in search of a vital centre, a primal wholeness and vigour, within the limits of Africa i.e., within his own psyche. As a white liberal, Gordimer has always found herself an outsider in her country. In her *The Late Bourgeois World* which had been banned in South Africa and got Nobel Prize in 1991, she has attacked apartheid. Gordimer knows that any form of slavery degrades oppressor as well as the oppressed. "It would be uncritical to study the works of Africans and non-Africans," says she, "without reference to each other and neither group has a monopoly on the truth."[4]

In Gordimer's fiction, her white characters are questing for their individual identity and their western-European selves as well. They are luckless Europeans who found only graves, not gain and glory in Africa. They all are taking a self-preservative flight into Exile, Isolation and Alienation. In one of her novels, *Occasion for Loving*, Jasse Stilwell insists on seeing herself as "intact alone."[5] James Bray, the Englishman, in *A Guest of Honour*, returned to Africa to set up a modern educational system in the country, "fades away behind the insect-stained windshield of the car carrying him to a violent death."[6] The Booker Prize winner novel *The Conservationist* is about the longing of Mehring, whom "no one'll remember where he is buried."[7]

From an overt concern with the dilemma of whites in a changing South African society, Gordimer shifts her focus in *My Son's Story* to the experience of coloured South Africans and their cross-social relationship. Like *Burger's Daughter*, *My Son's Story* is a novel of development. In the narrative, Gordimer also makes use of metafiction, which is apparent in both the title of the text and in the epigraph, taken from Shakespeare's sonnet 13: "you had a father, let your son say so." This tale, then, is a son's telling of both his own and his father's stories. The challenge, therefore, falls to the reader to trust the son to be a reliable narrator of both stories.

In the novel, Will recounts how his adulterous father, Sonny, betrays both his family and the resistance movement when he has an extramarital affair with Hannah Plowman, a white activist. Will's accidental discovery of the affair draws him both into his father's deceit and into the limited but safe harbour of storytelling. However, Will is also loyal to Aila, his mother and Sonny's wife; he also gradually assumes the central position in the family as they become increasingly involved in the resistance movement independently of Sonny. Worse yet, Sonny has lost touch with the family so greatly that state is able to destroy the unit before he realizes that they are at risk. In addition, he loses Hannah when she accepts a United Nation's position outside South Africa. Sonny's isolation and marginalization is significant. His ultimate condition speaks to the utter sufferings of the black community. Sonny's early orientation toward colonialism, his initial detachment from the anti-apartheid movement, his liaison with Hannah and his increasing loyalty to her at the expense of his family and the resistance indicate the conflict and dilemma of cross-racial relationship in *My Son's Story*. However, the need for personal and political commitment of the idea of the healthy and unified state is also a hidden message of the novel.

In the novel the narrator is not established as a black but as a member of the 'coloured' community, which occupies a kind of 'middle condition' between those of the blacks and the whites. This symbolizes the split situation of Nadine Gordimer herself. She is by race and upbringing white, by conviction of the black cause. To Will, it offers the possibility for maximum contemplation. He is in a position to experience both the false sense of superiority of the whites and the outcast sense of being black, but also to regard both blacks and whites as 'other.' It also stands for the divided vision of South Africa.

The novel depicts the active involvement of 'coloured community' in the freedom movement. The father Sonny is a liberation leader who became involved with the woman, a human rights worker, when in prison. The affair continues, causing suppressed tension among all members of Sonny's family. The son, Will, who is struggling to reach sexual maturity, is filled with bitterness against his father. Will's sister Baby takes drugs, attempts suicide, then finally leaves home to join the armed struggle. Surprisingly, when the security police at last raid the family home, it emerges that even Sonny's wife, the shy and submissive Aila, has become a freedom fighter.

Like E.M. Forster's *A Passage to India*, *My Son's Story* also indicates that once black and white stand on the same level, only then will healthy cross-racial relationship became possible: until then they remain complicit in the false consciousness which racial taboo engenders. Furthermore, it is Baby and Aila who most readily make the saving transition into involvement with the cause. Even Sonny and Hannah whose relationship was forged out of their political activism move tentatively to a less sterile relationship, that of "common goal outside self"[8] under the stress of Aila's arrest and trial.

Nadine Gordimer has for many years been a great and gallant keeper of the white South African conscience. She continues to fulfil this role in *My Son's Story*. At the same time there are hints in this new novel that in the liberated South Africa both black and white could live in harmony. The end of racism was the realization of the dream of South Africans for equality. Now in the free nation the main task is to build a society in which all South Africans, black and white, would be able to prosper. The political freedom of the blacks of South Africa through a peaceful electoral process is the most significant event in the annals of human history for self-rule since the independence of India blazed a trail of departure of colonial powers from Asia and Africa. The case of South Africa is even more significant. Elsewhere on the continent the formal colonial masters withdraw to Europe. But the whites of South Africa who gracefully accepted a democratic dispensation, knowing full well the consequences of being a minority community, have earned the gratitude of all who value democracy. Of course, the credit goes to Gordimer who has already predicted and hoped for these circumstances in *My Son's Story*. The momentous choices that are made by Sonny,

Baby, Aila, Hannah, except Will, between private and public, are without apparent inner conflict. The characters stroll unaffected at any deep level through the crisis of their lives. This is to a large extent because Gordimer, engaged by the political struggle, has not been concerned to capture those inner lives which according to the logic of the narrative have been so affected by that struggle. The only little inner conflict we do see is in Hannah's reference to promotion above her relationship with Sonny. Undoubtedly, it is a reflection of the emancipated western woman. The novel is not entirely without its moments of tension, of heightened emotion, of insight into the complexity of the human condition, but it is perhaps appropriate for Gordimer to contemplate for a society having divided vision but at any cost unified.

The final 'event' in the narrative, the burning-down of Sonny's family home, can also be seen in this light. The temporary home of the native, which features prominently in several well-known postcolonial novels, serves both as a symbol of insecurity and displacement, and as a sign of a personal integrity and comparative well-being which is both contrasted with public degradation and to some extent infected by it. In *My Son's Story* the conflagration has a complex significance as well as being an act of white racism it serves as punishment of Sonny for his misdeeds. It also stands for the earlier break-up of the family. At one point Will observes, "Just like Dad. My sex life has no home." (185) But it is also a sign of hope for the future. And it brings the personal and the political togetherness of South African Community:

And then of course the old rhetoric took the opportunity. We can't be burned out, he said, we're that bird, you know, it's called the phoenix, that always rises again from the ashes. Prison won't keep us out. Petrol bombs won't get rid of us. This street this whole country is ours to live in. (276)

NOTES

1. O.R. Dathorne, *The Black Mind: A History of African Literature* (London: Heinemann, 1974), p. 211.
2. Nadine Gordimer, "Writers in South Africa: The New Black Poets," *Exile and Tradition—Studies in Africa and Caribbean Literature* (Rowland Smith, Longman, 1976).
3. Nadine Gordimer, "A Writer in South Africa," *The London Magazine*, 5, No. 2, 1965, p. 28.
4. J.A. Ramsaran, *New Approaches to African Literature* (Ibadan: Ibadan University Press, 1965), p. 35.
5. Nadine Gordimer, *Occasion for Loving* (New York: Viking, 1963), pp. 7-19.
6. Nadine Gordimer, *A·Guest of Honour* (New York: Viking, 1970), p. 423.
7. Nadine Gordimer, *The Conservationist* (Middlesex: Penguin, 1978), p. 177.
8. Nadine Gordimer, *My Son's Story* (Middlesex: Penguin, 1991), p. 224.